Living With Adult Children

Living With Adult Children

db

Diction Books
P.O. Box 17271
St. Paul, MN 55117

A Helpful Guide for Parents and
Grown Children Sharing
the Same Roof

Monica Lauen O'Kane

Illustrated by Jan Hosking

1st Printing, 5,000, 1981
2nd Printing, 7,000, 1982

ISBN 09609198-0-5 paperback

ISBN 09609198-1-3 hardcover

Dedication

This book is dedicated to my family.

First and foremost this book is dedicated to my husband, Hugh, for his encouragement towards my writing and for his understanding when the household didn't run quite on schedule.

This book also is dedicated to my children: Maureen, Kevin and his wife, Terry, Tracy, Patrick, Katie, Joe, Tom and Megan, who, by their words of wisdom, reminded me that life still goes on even when Mom is writing a book.

Often the reminder was soft and gentle. Sometimes Katie would hesitatingly approach me saying, "Uh, Mom, I hate to bother you, but could you French braid my hair?" Other times the reminder was quite blunt. One day 15-year-old Joe asked if I'd make him some hot cereal. I replied that maybe he could do this himself. His retort was, "Well, Mom, you're just going to have to decide if you want to be a mother or an author!"

Contents

Foreword

Much has been written about the chaotic change occurring in the American family. That change is occurring is quite evident to even the casual observer. Why those changes are occurring requires more thought, more reflection. Analyzing changes of family life in America in the later part of the 20th century requires an appreciation of the history of the family in many different cultural contexts in the recent and not so recent past. A good familiarity with the works of contemporary psychologists, social psychologists, and sociologists is also extremely helpful and necessary if one is to understand the myriad of changes at the societal, extended family, nuclear family and individual levels on the family.

Monica O'Kane has written a very thoughtful, much too brief, book on one aspect of the changing American family. Children that remain at home after completing high school and adult children that return to live at home for varying lengths of time is the focus of O'Kane's book. These nesters, as the author refers to the children in question, present many stresses and joys for all family members.

Monica O'Kane's multi-faceted analysis of this nesting phenomenon is carried out with respect to history, contemporary social science, and humor—a rare admixture. *Living With Adult Children* is a timely, very readable book that can provide usable strategies for parents and children in the midst of the nesting phenomenon. The chapters on communications, money matters and lifestyles particularly offer remedies to problems that the print media have worried about for several years.

Hopefully, Monica O'Kane will write more—on this and other related topics. We all need to better understand the forces impinging on the American family.

Roger J. Lauen, Ph.D.
Community Sociologist
Brother of the author

Preface

My husband and I have eight children, five of whom are adults. For the past eight years, we've had anywhere from one to four of these adult children living at home. The number is constantly fluctuating, but one thing is for sure— there's always at least one of them at home. Our eldest, Maureen, 26, has moved in and out so often that she calls herself "The Yoyo." No wonder some people term this "The Swinging Door Syndrome."

Because of our family situation, I wanted to read something informative about grown children who live at home. But I couldn't find any book written on the subject. I finally concluded that, to read the book, I'd first have to write it. And why not? After all, our family had plenty of first-hand experience! So I gathered all the available information—and it wasn't much. That convinced me to write this book.

Most of the published data had been written by professionals, who generally were working with troubled families who had come to them for counsel. But I wanted information about "normal" families, and set out to find it. A survey seemed the best way to get additional data. I sent a carefully worded, seven-page questionnaire to families in many geographical areas, with varying income levels, ethnic backgrounds, and family size. The only prerequisite for participation in the study was that the family have an adult child or children—age 18 or a high school graduate, whichever came later—living in the parental home.

Survey respondents showed a range as follows:

- Financial status: a combined parental income from $14,000 to $100,000 annually.

- Ethnic groups: Caucasian, Lebanese, Hawaiian, Black, Canadian, Mexican.

- Family size: from one to eleven children per family.

- Geographical area: Colorado, Florida, Hawaii, Illinois, Indiana, Iowa, Minnesota, New Jersey, New York, Ohio, and South Dakota.

I received more than one hundred completed surveys. Sixty had been filled in by one of the parents—most often by the mother, with one step-mother, and some fathers responding. Forty-two were completed by adult offspring, with five surveys being jointly filled in by both a parent and an offspring, and four completed by both parents together. In eight instances, both a parent and an adult offspring in the same family responded on separate questionnaires.

All questionnaire respondents have been given fictitious names, as have the people in the human interest stories used throughout the book. But they are real and alive—as real as your own family. The only true names used are public figures, such as television personality and talk show host, Phil Donahue, and families and persons who have appeared in newspaper or magazine articles.

It was a delight to read the completed surveys. They came from average, ordinary families trying to work out their situation of having a Full Nest. Reading the completed surveys, therefore, also gave me new encouragement. One mother even replied, "Your survey was interesting, and in answering it, Nellie (her daughter) and I became closer and more open with each other." Quotations from the surveys are sprinkled throughout the book in hopes of giving you, a glimpse of what I saw while reading them. Included in this book are examples of various situations from these families and their reactions to them. It is my belief that, with the examples of others who have made it work, this book will give encouragement and understanding to those families who have their adult children living at home.

I tried to be objective while writing this book, but because of our family experiences, I must admit to a slight bias. While this book is certainly not a definitive word on the subject of adult children living at home, I hope, at least, that it will be a worthy incentive to inspire further studies to help families in this area.

Last, but definitely not least, it must be added that my husband and I grew up in God-fearing homes and we are committed to a religious philosophy. It is only with the daily help of God that we can fulfill our duties as parents. Being spiritual doesn't mean there won't be problems. It does mean, however, that God will help us with them. We trust, rely on, and acknowledge our need for His help. On countless occasions, He has been our source of strength. Many times a day, an arrow-like prayer to heaven brings a quick response.

Acknowledgments

I wish to acknowledge the help of the following people for their assistance in writing this book:

The one hundred and ten questionnaire respondents added greatly to my store of knowledge and provided insights about nesting families.

Terry McDermott O'Kane, my daughter-in-law, helped me organize the material after I wrote the first draft of the text.

Tine Thevenin, author of *The Family Bed: An Age Old Concept in Child Rearing*, volunteered to read the manuscript. She offered countless valuable, common sense suggestions.

Mary Ann Fitzharris, editor and friend, gave the manuscript a light touch with her wonderful word editing. Incidentally, just a few short weeks after completing her portion of the work on this book, Mary Ann gave birth to her second child, another daughter.

Introduction

How delightful to find a book which addresses in such a positive manner the subject of adult children living with their parents! Just as mothers and fathers are encouraged to enjoy their infants and children and be sensitive to their needs, so also it is important to do likewise with adult members of the family. Monica O'Kane has thoroughly researched this heretofore little understood topic and presents her findings in an orderly, informal, easy-to-read style. With great understanding, she presents the case for the young adult living at home who is so often pressured by parents and society to "get out of the house and be on his own" at age 18 or so.

Monica's insights are invaluable in enlightening and encouraging parents when their offspring are in the process of making lifetime decisions. Underlying her exploration is the query: "After investing so much in our children, why not enjoy them on an adult level?"

Mary Ann Kerwin
Mother of eight (four now adults)
Founder and Board Chairman of
La Leche League International

Living With Adult Children

"Without a family, man, alone in the world, trembles with the cold."
—Andre Malraux[1]

CHAPTER I

The Full Nest Syndrome: An Unrecognized Phenomenon in Our Country

Before the 1930's, almost all of America's children left home only when they got married, enrolled in college, or went into the military service. It was the unusual person who left home without having a specific reason for doing so. Starting in the 1930's, however, there began a surge of young people who, upon reaching age 18, were off and out of the house. They were seeking independence, searching for themselves, or just getting out of an uncomfortable home situation. Thirty years later, the decade of the '60's saw the climax of this practice of getting out of the parental home as quickly as possible. This was, after all, the decade of independence from any and all authority. Now, more than twenty years later, those kids are parents too, and they add to the consecutive generation of adults who think it's unusual for a grown child (over 18) to live on in the parental home. In some instances, these people criticize other parents for allowing a grown child to live at home, and they also criticize the adult children living at home for refusing to become "independent." But it seems short-sighted to criticize such an age-old custom.

1

It is a typical occurrence that our collective memories don't seem to extend back any further than our own lifetimes. Yet, in past centuries and other cultures, it was common for all family members, regardless of age, to live in one home—grandparents, parents, and grandchildren. Generally there was no magical time when an individual had to move from his parents' home in order to be recognized as an adult. Even today, in a few pocket geographical areas, such as the Netherlands and Serbia, the Old World style of several generations living under one roof has persisted as the norm.[2] Now, in our Western world, this extended, multi-generational family is occurring once again—with a new twist. It's now adult grown children, many of whom had left home, who are returning to their parents' homes.

Between 1969 and 1980 the proportion of adult offspring living at home between the ages of 20 and 29 increased by 25 percent.[3] At the time of the 1980 United States Census, approximately 16 million adult offspring were living in their parents' home. This averages out to about 6 percent of the population, which is a considerable amount of people. With this surprisingly high number, it's certainly appropriate for us to re-examine the phenomenon of more young people cleaving unto their parents.[4]

Today, the Full Nest Syndrome, as some parents term it, is causing quite a sociological stir, and is raising a lot of questions. One assumption we can make is that traditionally, there have been certain informal regulations by which the family with adult offspring was ruled. But what are these guidelines? Have they been lost through the gap of the past 30-40 years when few grown children lived at home? How many other families besides yours and mine are therefore struggling by trial and error to make this recurring phenomenon work? Let us take a brief look at what scarce bit of information we can obtain from the past, then see what insights present-day families can give us, so we can rediscover some workable guidelines.

Kathryn, an acquaintance, related the following conversation that she overheard one day while shopping.

"Hi, Sally! What's new with you? Why it must be six years since we've last talked. Your kids must be all grown and gone by now."

"Grown? Yes," replied Sally. "But gone? No! They've all decided to live at home while going on with their schooling."

"What? School, I can understand. But why are they still at home?" was the aghast reply.

Many families with grown children living at home feel isolated, as if they were the only ones in this situation. But the above statement by Sally, simple as it is, is being repeated by parents all over the country. Slowly but surely, as the phenomenon increases, adult offspring living at home are "coming out of the closet," and discovering there are thousands of others in the same situation.

As the numbers of young people living at home increase, so do the numbers of parents who worry. They worry that by allowing their grown kids to live at home, they'll be encouraged never to leave, but instead stagnate forever in their birth place. However, our research shows that most young people will leave the parental home as soon as they are financially and emotionally able to do so. Some may have to come back temporarily one or more times. But it's really the exceptional individual who will stay on, and on, and on. Almost all live-in adult young people are there temporarily, not lifelong. In most cases, these offspring don't want to, or can't afford to set up their own households because of inflation, high education costs, expensive rent and utility bills, and other economic reasons.

What are the parents' motives for allowing the Full Nest Syndrome to occur? "Having a good family life" tops the list of objectives that 96 percent of Americans have set for themselves, according to a current Louis Harris Survey of 1,220 adults nationwide.[5] This clearly indicates just how very important family is to most people. But wanting, and having, are two different things. It takes a lot of hard work, concentration and caring to make a "good family life" come about, especially if one's family includes grown kids living at home. There are often financial and emotional conflicts, and family members have to make concessions. However, unique benefits also exist for those who make the effort to look for them. And benefits there can be! "We've discovered that we appreciate many of the same things," writes a father of his 29-year-old son living at home. "I find that I enjoy his company, his wit, and his intelligence. When he leaves I'll probably regret it."[6] In another family, the mother, who is a single parent, feels that it's less lonely, albeit more work and expense with her three grown children (ages 30, 25, and 18 years) living at home. We do need to stop once in a while to count our blessings, while we think about our problems and how to solve them.

What makes a child a child?

Children require a "warm, protected, and prolonged period of nurture," one writer said.[7] But it took people a long time to recognize this fact. Some periods in European history deemed the early years of a person's life so unimportant that the child was considered a non-person. Then there was a period when children were mixed with adults "as soon as they were considered capable of doing without their mothers or nannies, not long after a tardy weaning at about the age of seven years."[8] The child was regarded as a small adult who mingled, competed, worked and played with mature adults.

The peoples of primitive eras and ancient Greek times at least recognized a transition between the world of children and that of adults, a transition they celebrated by means of an initiation or an educational stage.[9] However, this was lost in time, and during the medieval centuries, life was either child's play or man's work, without much emphasis on the transition. It seems that for many children, recognizing this transition makes growth a little easier.

The acknowledgement of childhood as a separate stage of development grew slowly over the centuries. Then, finally various stages of childhood were acknowledged. It was not until the beginning of the 15th Century that the age of childhood was "discovered." In 1550 it was finally decided that there were three recognizable stages in a person's life: childhood, youth (which then meant the prime of life), and old age.[10]

During the 18th Century, adolescence was recognized as a transition from childhood to adulthood, in part, due to the fact that formal education was introduced. When children started attending school, this was the beginning of an understanding of the various stages of childhood. As schooling became more formal and extended, age division became more acute. At this time, growing stages became defined as infancy, childhood, adolescence, and young adulthood. As the centuries rolled along, the period of being a child was extended, and these various stages of childhood emerged and crystalized. Many people came to believe that children needed a prolonged dependency on their parents in order to have a healthy emotional development.[11]

However, this "great concern" ceases abruptly when the child reaches adulthood. It seems that when a child reaches 18 he is swallowed into adulthood and no longer gets the attention he still so urgently needs, no matter where he lives. One wonders why. Surely there is a need for data on this stage of a person's life. We have now come to the time in history where we should acknowledge one more stage of development—the time of transition from adolescence to the total self-supportive stage. For some, this is an important phase of development.

Upon reflection, it is quickly evident that there is no specific word for the grown child who lives at home. What should we call this person? "Child" won't do, for surely he isn't! "Offspring" is too awkward and is not a readily used or common term. "Grown child" seems too clumsy. We have a name for every other age group: embryo, fetus, infant, baby, toddler, pre-schooler, child, adolescent, teen, juvenile, young person. And then it jumps to adult. Surely, with the vast array of words in our language, we should have a label for these over 18, transition-age young adults. If we remember, though, that the practice of living at home has only recently become an issue of concern, we can see that there was never a need for a term for this group of grown children who live in the parental home.

But times are changing and so we move along with the times and coin a new word—"nester"; by definition, "an adult offspring living in the parental home."

A more in depth definition of the nester is a young adult straddling youth and adulthood with one foot in the world of dependency and the other foot taking searching steps into independency.

Defining the Family

Originally, the word family meant "dweller in a household." According to Webster's dictionary, family now means a "group of persons consisting of two parents and all their children." Today, many professionals enlarge the concept of family to mean a "group of persons living under the same roof, including both those actually related by blood, and all the others (dependents and friends), forming the household." For the purpose of this book, the meaning of family will be parents and children, *regardless of age*, related by blood or adoption living in the same household.

For a more in depth description of the concept of "family" as relating to nesters, let's examine its commonly accepted responsibilities. The family provides food, shelter, protection, security, and emotional support to its members. According to columnist Ellen Goodman, "The family is formed not for the survival of the fittest, but for the weakest. It is not an economic unit, but an emotional one. This is not the place where people ruthlessly compete with each other, but where they work for each other. Its business is taking care, and when it works, it is not callous but kind...We don't have to achieve to be accepted by our families. We just have to be. Our (family) membership is not based on credentials but on birth."[12]

Parents should teach their children how to function in the world outside the family. Home is a training ground that prepares the child to exist apart from the family in later life. Most offspring in the animal world are ready to live life apart from their parents at a relatively early age. Not so with human offspring. They require a period of growth, commonly considered to be 18 years, before they are ready to leave the nest and function apart from the family. However, millions of grown children are finding that it takes longer than 18 years. And in this world far from the simple life of farmer, baker, and cabinetmaker of pre-1900, some professionals even see the maturing process extending past age 30. Daniel Levinson, Ph.D., a pioneer in the study of adult development, feels that the whole process of entering adulthood lasts from about age 17 to age 33![13]

Nesters need to feel welcomed, loved, and encouraged during this time of transition. The parental home, however humble it may be, seems to naturally fulfill these needs. Often the nesters leave and return, then leave again only to return once more. The periods of time away from the parental home gradually become increasingly longer until the homecoming falls into a new category: a visit.

"The study of the family is in large part the study of how people have come to terms with the basic facts of life—not only with mating, child-bearing, and child-rearing, but with work and play, *as well as with survival in a sometimes hostile environment* and with the critical changes that come with aging and with death," according to one set of authors.[14]

In order to meet the particular needs of its members, families have devised all sorts of living arrangements, such as everyone living together in one house, rural children living with city relatives, and apartment living for more established, older children. Families differ, though, because the needs of its members differ. Some grown children are able to function on their own outside the family home, but some need more time with their parents. The family with nesters is a response to grown children who still want, or need, to live in the parental home.

The relationship between parents and their children is, for the most part, the closest, most intimate association people experience outside the marriage bond. Up until the present, professionals have written volumes about the interaction between parents and their young children. But today there is a need to extend the literature to cover the relationship between parents and their adult offspring. After all, we spend the greater part of our total life as adults. Relating to each other as one adult to another adult is a totally different relationship than adult to child. This new relationship brings both benefits and problems. One writer describes it thus: "In real life...living under one roof produces as much misery as joy, but a good deal of both."[15]

Another writer feels that if a family can work out its problems and enjoy the benefits of grown children living in the parental home, they will know an extra fullness to life. Man was not meant to live alone, for he is a social creature. Sharing life with others gives us great happiness, and of course our happiness is magnified when we can share our lives with those persons who are our own adult offspring.[16]

Family Types

There are several ways of labeling families, but two categories that most sociologists agree on is the nuclear and traditional families. Roget's *Thesaurus* gives the definition of nuclear as: "center, heart, core, kernel, basis, or foundation." The nuclear family, therefore, generally consists of a husband, wife and their minor (under age 18) children. The traditional family consists of the nuclear group, plus other family members in need of a home.

The Traditional Family. Families of this type take in the young, the old, and the needy. In this setting, an elderly grandparent, a homeless niece, or a grown son or daughter is welcome anytime at home. This family is receptive, responsive, and especially open to the needs of their children, whatever their age. Because of their acceptance of kindred responsibilities and commitments, these parents are willing to submerge their own feelings for the greater benefit of the whole family. They do this out of a sense of loyalty, feeling that they want to share their home and lives with those who want to live with them. If one person is in need of special care and loving support, either on a short- or a long-term basis, be it financial, emotional or physical, he is given all that the family can give.[17] Certain needs can best and sometimes only be met by the immediate family. The self-orientated, individualistic, "I'm for me" attitude prevalant in our present society, makes a traditional family exceptional in this day and age.

Now, when 16 million adult offspring are living in the parental home, the family is being asked to extend itself a little further and for a longer period of time than some parents had originally intended. Millions of families have risen to this challenge. Often, however, this causes emotional and financial conflicts. Compromises have to be made by everyone. But the traditional family with nesters changes and develops, as do the individual family members who are involved. In the process, they are discovering areas of strength that possibly they didn't know were there.

The John Kneebone family is one of our present-day traditional families. Mr. Kneebone, a 59-year-old grocer from Boulder, Colorado, says, "Five of our seven children, ages 15, 17, 23, 26, and 30, still live at home. The other two live nearby. We've always been a very close family. None of the kids has ever given us any real problems—like with drugs and alcohol. We've done things together since they were very young. The only hard thing now is getting everyone free from work at the same time so that we can take a vacation together."[18]

One woman in the audience of the Phil Donahue Show reflected the attitude of a traditional family when she stated, "I feel that there is no age that you can shut the door and lock it (keeping out your grown children)." This was met with applause from the audience.

A mother of ten children, with one grown child and five younger children currently living at home, related, "My relatives regard the home as a permanent living place until marriage and are horrified if anyone suggests moving out before it is absolutely necessary. When our second child, a daughter, turned 18 and was going to move out, Grandmother insisted that she live with her, thereby continuing a 'family living' pattern. Surprisingly and happily, the 18-year-old was delighted to live at Grandma's house even under the watchful eye and curfew rules which were the same as at our home."

One parent said that she hopes her younger children, "having seen the older ones who remain at home, will feel that they too are welcome to stay when they reach adulthood, no matter what the current trends are toward moving out when they reach 18."

The Nuclear Family. Today, traditional, extended family living has gone out of vogue. In pursuit of better jobs, families are moving more often than in times past, and this further disrupts relations among family members. Distance between families are growing, and family ties have weakened. So, gradually, the smaller, nuclear family is replacing the traditional, extended family, and kids are growing up not knowing their cousins, aunts, uncles—and even grandparents.

The nuclear family that has evolved in the more advanced and affluent Western societies characteristically takes a different view of its responsibilities. The goal is generally the greatest comfort of each of its members, and it tries to find a course of action that is best for all concerned. It frequently calls in outside professional advice, and often is eager to abdicate its caretaking function to outside authorities. Everybody goes out, or is taken out periodically, for treatment by doctors, dentists, orthodontists, psychiatrists and family consultants, and on their recommendation a family may pack off difficult or hopeless cases to institutions for periods ranging from a few hours to the remainder of a lifetime. In fact, the proliferation of kindergartens, day-care centers, hospitals, asylums and retirement homes is one of the characteristics that distinguishes modern Westen society from all other societies past and present.

In such institutions efficient, bureaucratic care replaced, or is supposed to replace, the generally affectionate and well-intentioned but perhaps slap-dash methods of relatives ministering to their kin in private dwellings. What the new method gains in efficiency, it may lose in the human warmth provided by an old-fashioned family in an old-fashioned home.[19]

The nuclear family faces isolation, having only two adults to share the burdens. Some historians feel that the nuclear family is presently in a further state of transition and decay, since even the family members are becoming isolated from each other. They spend so little time with each other because both parents are working outside the home and the children spend their hours in day-care centers or schools. Fathers, who once held authority and were seen as the family's pillar of strength, now stand in want of some respect from their children. Family ties which were once strong now are weak with lack of communication even between the immediate members of some families. Perhaps the constant mobility of families stands to blame.

To nest or not to nest, that is the question.

In some families, no home is big enough to house two generations, for lack of room or tolerance. So, the young are exhorted to "go west," go to college—in short, get out.[20]

Sometimes these feelings are right out front, but often they are submerged deep in the subconscious and are difficult to admit. One father on the Phil Donahue Show was finally able to verbalize his feelings on the subject. Here are excerpts from that conversation:

" 'I feel the parents' responsibility is to make sure kids are educated. Make sure that if they have a problem, or really have trouble, that they are able to come home. But at the time their education is finished, my kids understand they're moving out. I don't think two families can live together,' the father stated.

" 'Once they get the baccalaureate,' Phil started to question, 'once they graduate...'

" 'The father interrupted, 'They're on their own!'

" 'Write them off the hook?' Phil asked.

" 'Yeah,' the father responded. 'Once they move out of my house, from under my control, they're cut off. And they know it.'

" 'It's clear that you've come a long way without my advice; but just for the sake of our conversation,' said Phil, 'I sense in you and in lots of other men around the country an authoritarian attitude, which says, 'This is the way it is and this is my house.' Is this the kind of attitude that opens dialogue, understanding, friendship, and caring between fathers and sons, mothers and daughters, parents and kids? If we are sustaining real pain in many households across the country because of people who don't share feelings, is it possible that this judgemental attitude is at the bottom of this inability to communicate?'

" 'I *have* had a little difficulty communicating with my daughter, in fact,' admitted the father."[21]

(Author's comment: This father may just have realized that his lack of communication may well have been one of the contributing causes of his unyielding attitude toward his children.)

Phil continued on the topic and indicated that in our present culture there seems to be prevailing negative attitude toward intimate relationships which carry responsibilities. "It looks like we can't wait to get rid of each other....We can't wait to get separated."[22]

There's no set rule about whether or not it's best for adult offspring to live with their parents. Even in our culture we have variations in family living arrangements. One adult offspring phrased it thus, "I don't feel it's a question of what you should do or what you shouldn't do (nesting or not). It's what's right for you and your parents. Personally I don't agree with the idea of living at home at the age of 30. But, you know, for some it's okay. It depends on their relationship."[23]

The decision of whether an adult offspring should nest or not depends a lot on the current capabilites of the parent. Violet Arnold, a Minneapolis psychotherapist, told of how one day her grown daughter telephoned her and said she wanted to move back home—again. She had been in and out many times previously. This time, however, Violet felt that she just would not be able to handle a return move. So she told her daughter, "Let's have lunch together and talk about it." Violet felt that they wouldn't be able to get too emotional in a public place. Over a bowl of soup, she told her daughter, "I love you very, very much, but I am not, at this time, able to handle your moving back home." Fortunately tears were spared and understanding reigned. Credit is due to both of them for that. Her daughter accepted her mother's statement and said she still loved her mom anyway. And, in turn, Violet found other ways to give her daughter the emotional support she wanted and needed.

Certainly not all adult children should or do live at home. Some grown children don't need to nest. They have managed to become independent, so they have no need or desire to live with or receive financial support from their parents. And not every family is able to house all their grown children who need a home. These parents may not have the finances, space or stamina needed to allow their grown children to live at home. Some individuals voiced their opinions on this topic. "I believe having an adult offspring in the home is a good thing when the relationship is productive, tension-free and happy," writes one nester, "but if this isn't possible, if things can't be worked out, it's best to separate." Another young adult puts it a little stronger, "I do not live at home and I would not live at home. Really, I didn't enjoy living at home. I pretty much had my freedom when at home, but I didn't like it. My mother and I just drove each other crazy!"

Children would rather move out if the home situation is not ideal—when for example, one of the parents is an alcoholic, or when there is a case of severe friction between the parents themselves. Sadly, sometimes home is just too painful a place to live, and it's best to leave. One woman with an alcoholic husband wrote that all of their children left home immediately after graduating from high school.

Some grown children who live outside the parental home still need help in order to be able to do this—usually in the form of regular or occasional financial assistance. One mother related, "Christie (her grown daughter living in an apartment) has been unemployed for three months. Never once did she ask to come back home, because she was striving for independence. She did, however, ask me to pay a utility bill for her, which I did." Some parents who are unable to accommodate their adult offspring in their home choose instead to help them with loans or gifts of money.

One mother felt there should be a limit to the length of time a grown offspring lived at home. "While I would want a 25-year-old to be out on his own," wrote one mother, "I'd like to see an 18-year-old stay at home for another few years." This mother had three nesters, ages 25, 20, and 18.

Conclusion

So now we have a new phenomenon in our society—the Full Nest Family. It appears that this type of family living is on the increase. Society is being confronted with the need to take the Full Nest Family seriously. There are various reasons why some offspring are nesting, resulting in specific problems and benefits. Historians recognize two types of families—traditional and nuclear. It is the former who are more apt to house a nester. Many of these families are looking for constructive guidance to help them because, although extended family living was common in past times, it is a new phenomenon in our lifetime.

"Early departure from the homestead is a moral crisis that many of our youth do not show themselves able to meet. It comes at a tender age, when judgement is weakest and passion and impulse strongest."
—An anonymous 18th Century advocate of keeping children at home longer than was customary.[1]

CHAPTER II

Nesters in Past Centuries and Other Cultures

A long backward glance into former times shows many examples of extended family living. Through the centuries, families have always had adult members remaining at home. At times, this was the result of grown children who didn't want to, or were unable to, set up their own households. In a few cultures they were even traditionally bound to live in the parental home.

When seen in historical perspective, we can certainly view living-in as customary and ordinary. Peter Laslett, a social historian, says it well when he calls this "understanding ourselves in time," for understanding history is the key to understanding the present.[2]

Extended Households in Europe. Extended family living was very common in Europe from the earliest centuries until the Industrial Revolution. There was not much privacy, as you can well imagine, since these households included a lot of people—grandparents, parents, and children. This was intense family living to its fullest: food, slumber, and recreation had to be shared in common. All family members

17

had no choice but to participate in the fine art of sharing, as do full nest families in our day.

The reasons for this type of multi-generational family living was much the same as today—economic recession, the burden of taxation, and its method of assessment. There was also one added element—depopulation as an aftermath of the Black Death or plague, for many of the breadwinners in the families were stricken and died, leaving families destitute and forced to live together. Often the grandfather and his eldest son worked the family farm. Subsequent sons either stayed single and remained on the family farm, or were "paid a sum of money (as their inheritance) by the eldest son to go off on their own."[3]

Extended living was common in some countries even in recent times. In a 1956 survey of 10,000 rural homes in 23 communities in Serbia, 26 percent were extended families, with some communities having as many as 55 percent and even 62 percent extended family homes.

Historian Laslett states that frequently persons living in such close relationships with others developed an ability for "intense communication" both among themselves, and with their communities. Thus, one can easily suppose that living together like this would certainly develop an intimate relationship among family members.

Poverty in the Netherlands and Serbia. In 18th century Holland, custom dictated that people could marry only when they were able to support a family. Those who couldn't afford this luxury stayed single and lived out their lives in their parents' homes. In many cases, if a family had more than one son, only one was able to get married and he wasn't able to do so until he was older. Unmarried daughters also stayed on in the family home.[4]

So the extended household evolved. In the province of Overijssel, there were 7,763 households in the year 1749 and 20.5 percent were extended family homes. The percentage was a bit higher in the rural areas (22.6 percent) than it was in the villages (15.3 percent).[5] Even in recent times, in the eastern part of the Netherlands during the early 1950's, 25 percent of farms were being worked by a family living with one of the married partner's parents.[6] It is still common for Dutch offspring to live at home until they are finished with their education at about the age of 25 years.

In 19th Century Serbia, the population was multiplying and land began to fill up. Economic and social competition developed since mass migration still hadn't occurred in this country, as it had elsewhere throughout Europe. The multi-generational household flourished. In many families, several married sons joined together with their fathers in living and working together. After the father's death, several brothers and their families continued to live on in the same home.

In parts of Yugoslavia today, farm households are extremely large. The limited availability of land or other economic opportunity, combined with a normal increase in population, continues to enlarge the size of individual modern farm households, for the children still have nowhere else to go.[7] Some current households are remarkably large. For instance, the household of Bajram Bujari contained sixty persons in 1958, with everyone (except the spouses) being descendants of Bajram's own grandfather. Needless to say, this type of family living requires a patriarch with a respected authority, in order to insure the smooth functioning of the household.[8]

The extended families were in a good position to multiply their property and become economically secure, because of their manpower.[9] Even so, when economic conditions are kinder and money is more readily available, people seem to prefer to live separately in small nuclear family units,[10] but usually still in close geographical location.

But today, as in the past, many people are feeling the financial pinch, especially our young people. Many grown children can't afford to live away from the family home. Our tolerance for the nester, therefore, should be based on historical perspective. It has been done before!

Sexual Maturity and Marriage Age in Europe and America.
One of the perplexing problems of the nester today is the
ever widening gap between sexual maturity and sexual
fulfillment in marriage. Studies of the last 100 years indicate
that children are maturing at an increasingly earlier age,
while at the same time young adults are marrying later and
later. Some countries have long kept extensive records of
the age of onset of menstruation. Thus we know that our
children are maturing sooner as time goes on. The following
table shows a decrease in the average age of onset of
menstruation.[11]

Table 1: Maturation Ages

Country	Maturation Age Then	Maturation Age Now
Norway	1850: 17.1 years	1951: 13.5 years
Sweden	1905: 15.7 years	1949: 14.1 years
United States	1904: 14.1 years	1951: 12.9 years

The above figures are median ages only. This means that
as many girls began menstruation before these dates as
after. The author is personally familiar with two girls whose
age at onset of menstruation was eight and nine years
respectively. Yet one other girl was 17 years old at onset of
menstruation.

The exception to the above norms of maturation were the
children of the well-to-do in 19th Century Europe. They
matured at an earlier rate than the children of the poor. This
meant greater physical achievement at an earlier age for the
wealthy, giving them yet another advantage over the poor.
There was a difference of 3.5 inches in height and 11.5
pounds in weight between the poorest working class boys
and the best off working class boys in York, England, in
1899. "The privileged, wealthy children must have been
taller, heavier, better developed and earlier to mature than
the rest; the males must have had beards and broken voices

much sooner, the women must have become full women much more quickly."[12] So the children of the rich matured sooner and gained physical strength sooner than did the children of the poor. But the average overall ages of sexual maturation in 19th Century Europe were about 3.5 years later than present day figures.

The picture thus emerges of children becoming sexually mature earlier than their parents, but having to wait a longer period before marriage. Current social and educational problems are forcing our young people to marry later and later, causing another social problem: sexually active, unmarried kids. Also, because they are marrying later, many of these young people are living in the parental home.

Over the centuries, the age at which young people customarily married has fluctuated. The later they married, the longer single children stayed at home with their parents. There were many reasons for people marrying later. The Medieval English, 19th Century Americans, and Irish of all generations give us striking examples of this.

Most young people of Medieval England waited until their middle twenties before considering marriage. This is late even by our present-day American standards, but exceptionally late when we consider these people had a life expectancy of 48 once they reached adulthood.[13]

When Medieval English young men reached marriage age, they were unable to wed until they had a nest egg to launch their new family. "When a son got married he left the family of his parents and started a family of his own," writes Peter Laslett about Medieval England. "If he was not in a (good financial) position to do this then he could not get married, nor could his sister unless the man who was to take her for his bride was in a position to start a new family."[14] A few wealthy Medieval English young women married at an early age, between 13 and 15 years, for they matured early and had the financial means to wed. It is interesting to note that in the play "Romeo and Juliet," Shakespeare convincingly put Juliet's age at 14, for she was one of the privileged wealthy class.

Traditionally, there were a lot of curtailments pertaining to marriage. For example, throughout the generations, even until today, the traditional family in Ireland stays together for a long time. Upon his marriage, a son is entitled to a property settlement. If there is no property to inherit, he may have to stay single until he accumulates some means to support a wife and family. This can take decades, or in some cases the money is never accumulated, thus making him ineligible for marriage. Lack of hard cash in farming families makes it difficult or even impossible for fathers to pay sons a salary on the family farm. If the son is to inherit the estate from his father, he will generally have to wait until his father is good and ready to retire and hand it over. Then when the father feels it is time, he and his wife move into a smaller bedroom and the son and his wife take the best bedroom, along with the title to the farm. It sometimes happens that the son has to wait so long that he becomes a confirmed bachelor and loses the inclination to marry.[15] Younger sons, knowing that the inheritance will go to the eldest, often leave the family farm and migrate to the city for employment.

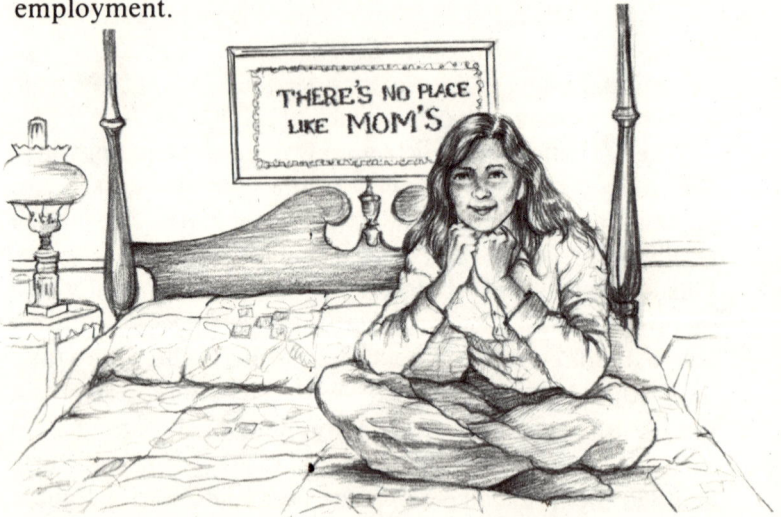

*Today, as in the past, many adult children remain at home for financial reasons. For some, there's no way to have a stereo, a car, nice clothes, **and** an apartment.*

Family Affection in 19th Century America. Throughout the years, for some nesters it has always been affection among family members which kept them at home. Parents and children just enjoyed each other and wanted to live together. Lasch and Taylor write that the American family in the 1840's lost its economic function (because people no longer grew their own food), and their educational function (because schools taught their children.)[16] So, the families that held together did so no longer out of need, but out of affection.

President Thomas Jefferson, widowed early, felt that he was a vagrant father throughout his official life. He tried through letters to guide his motherless daughters. Upon his retirement, he moved back to his home in Monticello and his daughter, Martha, and her family moved there, as they always did when the president was there from Washington. Martha was her father's companion during his later years. It was certainly affection that held this family together and made their life meaningful.[17]

Like the Jefferson's, and countless other families throughout the ages, many nesters in our day live in the parental home because they want to, saying that it's a happy, loving period that they and other family members enjoy.

Dictatorial Parents in the Iroquois Indian Tribes and Ancient Rome. Nesters who feel that they have little freedom because of an authoritarian or dictatorial parent may find comfort in taking a look backward to the Iroquois Indians. "When an (Iroquois) mother felt that her son was ready to marry, somewhere around the age of 22, she sought out a young woman who she thought he might like. The two mothers met and arranged a wedding date. Often the two young people didn't know about the marriage until a day or two before the wedding. It would have been considered disrespectful for the young couple to protest their mothers' decision."[18]

Some nesters today complain of parents who are interferring, but few parents today go to this extent.

Today's nesters who chafe at their authoritarian fathers might feel less irritated if they delved into history and discovered the "Poppa Power" of Ancient Rome. The father had complete control over his children and his son's children. After birth, the infant was placed at his father's feet. If he picked the baby up, it became part of the family. If he did not, this meant rejection, with subsequent disposal by the side of the road to die or to be taken away by a stranger, perhaps as a slave. Even after a son was grown and married, his father controlled his money and his property. He could arrange for his children's divorce, with or without their consent. His authority was so far-reaching that if he thought he had cause, he could even sell his son. However, this was hardly ever done. His power over his children extended even to death, for he had the authority, vested in him by government, after conferring with other family members, to condemn any of his children to death. This was rarely done though, as it was frowned upon by society.[19]

To be sure, some of our current nesters feel that they have a dictatorial or authoritarian father, but seen in comparison to Ancient Rome, our nesters' situation may look rather mild.

Married Nesters in China and the Maya Indian Tribes. Down through history we have examples of married children living in the parental home. Some countries had strong traditions which dictated how and where the newly married couple would live.

In China, the son was the nester, for he remained at home even after marrying, bringing his bride into his parents' home. Through long-standing custom, the new bride was chosen by her husband from a different village or part of the city. She then lived in her husband's parents' household, which was dominated by the fierce figure of her mother-in-law. Customarily, the mother-in-law humiliated the new bride—a tradition which was handed down from generation to generation, breeding misery and resentment. Each bride, in turn, repeated the cycle when she became a mother-in-law. Pressures became so intense that the suicide rate among females in the 21 to 30 age group was thirty-one times as great as it was among males.[20] The new bride had to be totally subservient to her husband, father-in-law, and mother-in-law. She was forced to be obedient and affectionate. In addition, her role as daughter-in-law took precedent to her role as wife.

Things got a little better when another son married and brought home a wife. The first wife then had seniority and status and the new wife was at the bottom of the totem pole. However, things did not improve noticeably until the mother-in-law died, for then the wife of the eldest son was the first woman of the house and could force the wives of other sons to do her bidding.[21]

When Geraldine Rhoads, editor of *Woman's Day* magazine, was traveling in China in the summer of 1980, she found that the editors of a comparable women's magazine in China considered one of the more common personal problems there to be mothers-in-law. She writes that it is still customary for a Chinese bride to live with her husband's family. Their houses and apartments are tiny by our standards, and close quarters certainly create even more friction. Grandparents mind the children while mothers and fathers work during the day.[22]

The Mayans in the 10th Century in Central America also accommodated the newly married couple in the parental home. This society was matrilocal, meaning that newly married couples lived in the bride's family home, but only on a temporary basis of five years. The new groom was expected to present a gift to his father-in-law, live in his home, and work for him during those years. This time may well have been used to acquire knowledge for later independent living. After the five compulsory years in the bride's parental home, the entire community celebrated by joining together and building a new house for the young couple.[23]

There are indications that married children and their families are returning to the parental home in ever-increasing numbers in our day. One realtor reports that she is now seeing at least one family grouping (nuclear family plus married child with family) per week that wants to buy a home together. Many of these present-day joint householders find that if they work out details in advance regarding chores, finances, and a projected date when the married nesters plan to move, then this can be a time of economic and emotional growth.

Single-Parent Nesters in Japan until the 14th Century. With an ever-increasing rate of single parents in our present day, it is understandable that a certain percentage do live in the parental home. For them, it might be interesting to be aware of a cultural tradition on this subject in another country.

The situation of a Japanese wife in many ways is very similar to our present-day, single-parent nester. Customs in Japan differed from other cultures in that, up until the 14th Century, a Japanese wife remained with her own family, her husband only visited her at night. He did not live with her. The Japanese word for marriage meant "to slip by night into the house!" So, for that period in history, prior to the 14th Century, the daughter was a nester and she lived in her parents' home, raising her children there without the daily support or company of a husband or a father for her children.[24] The grandparents, though, were able to support the wife and give guidance to the grandchildren.

Family Affluence in the Trobriand Islands. Life was easy for the Trobrianders, a group of people living in the southwest corner of the Pacific Ocean. They made their living with a minimum of effort by harvesting yams out of the jungle and reaping the vast benefits of the sea. The Trobriand children formed a body, a group apart, separate from the adults, much like our young teenagers. Often this group of young people were in opposition to their parents. They "led a happy, free, arcadian existence, devoted to amusement and the pursuit of pleasure," indulging freely in love affairs.[25] They were not expected to do any work and so they didn't. This hardly prepared them for the adult responsibilities of caring for a family. However, Trobriand parents discovered that eventually, their children did settle down into stable family life, just as their parents did before them.

Paul Kingsley, a California psychiatrist, feels that we may not be helping our young people assume adult responsibility as well as we could. He feels that our offspring grow up not knowing what is expected of them and thus are unprepared to accept adult responsibility. Some children turn eighteen and are told, "You are now legally an adult." They are then pushed out into life without much preparation.[26] However, even with this lack of direction at age 18, almost all offspring do generally follow in their parents' lifestyle sooner or later.

Conclusion

Through this brief historical and cultural scan, it becomes quite apparent that nesting is not unique or unusual. Extended family living was and is common in many cultures, and has been throughout the centuries. Poverty, a later marrying age, affection, need for emotional support, or affluence are all reasons why grown children have remained in the parental home. Certainly these same reasons apply with equal validity today. Factors such as a dictatorial parent can make this a difficult situation. However, there are many benefits in extended family living, such as the opportunity to save money. Viewed in historical perspective, we can see that nesting can be considered common, ordinary and usual. Indeed, understanding history really is the key to understanding the present.

"One night my husband and I sat down and tried to figure out what the attractions of living at home are — other than free laundry, free rent, free toiletries, security, love, a permanent address for mail, unlimited storage, financing and loans, convention rooms for private parties and entertaining, and guest privileges."[1]
—Humor columnist, Erma Bombeck

CHAPTER III

Attractions and Problems of Nesting

Let's examine the reasons why present-day grown sons and daughters are living in the parental home. Some are nesting out of desire — mom and dad's place is where they want to live. Others are there out of need: financial, emotional, and social. By analyzing nesters' many motives, hopefully your family may see some parallels in your own lives that may help you understand your own situation more fully.

Some young adults nest out of desire.

Some nesters are in the parental home out of desire — they just want to live there. These nesters, and their families, see many benefits to living together.

"Our adult children are living at home because that is where they like to live and we love to have them," writes one mother with three adult offspring and several younger children at home. "We have built many memories together.

29

We (my husband and I) hear the joy and laughter of our children ring throughout the house and feel we are truly blest."

One 31-year-old nester writes that she enjoys the physical comforts of living at home. She also appreciates the parental love and friendship, and the monetary savings. She writes, "We (she and her parents) have a mutually respectful adult relationship with each other." She does qualify her remarks by saying, "But if the situation were not good at home, I would modify my finances and live elsewhere."

The *New York Times* report on married children living at home mentions that some families experience a "warmer sense of belonging and closeness' at a time of widespread personal alienation."[2] Living together seems to foster feelings of loyalty by strengthening the ties that bind.

A 23-year-old Army veteran says that he can't find any good reason for leaving home. "My hometown area is great and the family is full of love." He relishes his mother's good home cooking. He appreciates the laundry that is neatly folded. He's grateful for a place to store all his belongings. Also not having the burden and expense of maintaining his own household is extremely attractive to him.

"Apartment living would be lonely," writes a 19-year-old female living at home. Also in the family, besides her parents, are two adult sisters, and two younger siblings. "I feel this (living together) enriches the family unit and makes for a happy, jolly home life. We're just not ready to leave the family home yet."

One mother of three nesters feels that her young adults support each other. She relates that two of her nesters like to keep an eye on their 21-year-old sister, who is a bit rebellious, and sometimes uses marijuana and alcohol to excess.

Some nesters are living at home partly because of the protection it offers from overzealous suitors. One female nester feels that, because she lives at home, it is easier to say "no" to an insistent date. Just the implied threat that he may encounter her father tends to dampen a young man's ardor. But young damsels are not the only victims. Not one, but several male nesters also appreciated this protection from overzealous companions. One 32-year-old bachelor was especially dismayed at the forward actions of various female friends who came to visit him in his apartment. He said this never happened when he lived at home.

Some young adults nest out of financial need.

One of the most common reasons that nesters cited for living at home was economic:

- "I can't afford to live outside the parental home."
- "I do not want to experience a drop in my scale of living."
- "Home is nicer than any apartment that I could afford to rent."
- "Adult offspring living at home have fewer financial worries."

Almost all nesters say that at least one of their reasons for nesting is economic hardship — making this the most important advantage to living at home. The old saying is, "Two can live as cheaply as one." Well, it follows that three can live just about as cheaply as two — or almost. It's certainly true that adding one more person to a household isn't nearly as expensive as one person living singly and paying the bills alone. Many young people are finding it increasingly difficult to be financially independent. They really need and appreciate the assistance of their parents: free or minimal room and board, loans or gifts, either regular or sporadic.

Some young adults nest to save money.

Even though 90 percent of the nesters stated that they are living at home because of economic hardship, 51 percent reported that while living at home they were saving money. Many had goals that they were striving to achieve.

It's generally cheaper for a young adult to live at home, even if he is paying room and board, since few nesters pay a

sum equal to what it would cost them to live in an apartment
or a home of their own. This often helps the nester to save
money for some specific purpose: a car, clothes, college
tuition, or down payment on a home. Several nesters
mentioned saving for a trip to Europe or other travels. One
nester is investing in art equipment, saying that he "wants
time to pursue creative interests without the responsibility
of independent living." Another nester, a 25-year-old male,
is investing in real estate and stock. He borrowed $7,000
from his parents which he is paying back in monthly
installments, along with his room and board payments of
$80 a month.

Some young adults nest in order to form an adult relationship with their parents.

A stable, loving family relationship, on an adult-to-adult
level, provides support, permanence, and a strong
foundation for daily living. A decided advantage of nesting
is that parents and offspring have the opportunity of
building a relationship as one adult to another adult. Most
family members will spend the greater part of their lives
relating to each other as adults. One writer on the subject
says, "If you can establish a mutually respectful relationship
with your parents, you could, by staying on (in the parental
home) create a happy period when you and your parents can
enjoy one another as adults."[3] Nesters and their parents can
talk about the duties for which each will be responsible. This
won't be easy to do, but if such a discussion does take place,
all will be able to enjoy the nesting period to a greater
degree.

Often the burden of responsibility weighs heavily upon
parents as they struggle to do the "right" things in raising
their children. In our preoccupation with parental duties we
all tend to overlook or miss some of the rewarding aspects of
parenthood. It's so easy to forget to smell the daisies along
the way. But after our children have become adults, it's too

late to smell last year's daisies. It's also too late to do any significant changing or further training in our offspring. Instead, it's time to sit back and enjoy the results of our many years' labor. For some parents, it comes as a surprise that they can actually enjoy their adult children as individuals. They're surprised to find that they have much in common. And then, when a word or glance from their grown son or daughter triggers memories of days gone by, they often experience a warm glow of remembrance and a spontaneous chuckle. They find that now they can laugh together at yesterday's serious incident.

Some young adults nest for companionship.

Living together as a family provides many companionship advantages for both parents and nesters. In addition, there can be particular advantages for the parent in situations of a death of a marriage partner, a divorce, or in growing old.

One mother writes, "We especially like to have another adult besides us parents living at home because we can go out and feel safe about the younger children. Then, too, when my husband recently went on a fishing trip, I was glad to have Al, our 28-year-old, living here. I felt safe and not lonesome. During the six years that Al has lived at home as an adult, my husband sometimes worked nights and I was glad and appreciative to have another adult in the house. Moreover, I really appreciate the use of his car. He arranges to leave it for me whenever I need it."

A 25-year-old male nester relates that, after his father died, his mother needed help in raising the three younger children. He moved back home and his mother appreciated the support of an older male figure around the house.

One 26-year-old female nester has moved back home with her mother after her parents' divorce, and is now able to offer both emotional and financial support for the large family left at home. Her $125 monthly room and board augments her mother's insufficient income. "Rent is so steep," writes the nester, "that I don't want to be wasting my money by living alone in an apartment. I'd rather help to support the family at home."

In addition to the financial advantages for her, she loves the activity surrounding the family home. She claims she was lonely living in an apartment. Since it was cheaper for her to live at home, she was also able to start a savings account for an anticipated trip abroad.

Some elderly parents need assistance in daily chores. A nester who can help with the cooking, laundry, and shopping is a valuable asset in this special time of need. The nester can also be a companion to a parent who would otherwise be alone.

Nesters, as well as their parents, share the same advantages of companionship, especially in cases of illness or handicap, a traveling spouse, or a return from military services. There is an obvious advantage to living at home in these cases. The family is able to help this special nester with everyday living needs. Yet it is important that, as much as possible, a handicapped person be allowed and encouraged to be a contributing part of the family.

Sometimes there are two nesters: a married child and a spouse. Often nesting helps them save money. But, when one of the partners has to do a lot of traveling, or is required to work late hours, the spouse left at home appreciates the companionship of the family. And, the working spouse knows that even though he is not able to keep his mate company as often as he'd like, the family can fill in for him. One female nester is married to a Navy man, who is sometimes gone for months at a time away on cruise. She says, "I have no other appropriate person with whom to live. My husband is gone so long, that apartment living would just be too lonely!" Instead, by living with her parents, she can experience everyday companionship and a family spirit that is joyous, loving and generous—one which binds that family together.

Some returning veterans nest for a period of time. This is especially needed if he is emotionally or physically injured. This nester requires the loving support of his family to help him return to the life he had before, or to begin another one anew. John, one veteran who moved back home, responded to a call-in talk show. He said that he had developed a drug and alcohol addiction while in the military service and was happy to move into the safety of his parents' home. "It was good to know," he said, "that my folks were there to welcome, accept and help. This meant so much to me!"[4]

Some young adults nest in order to mend relationships.

Oftentimes a child's adolescent years are emotionally trying to both parents and child. Things are said and incidents happen that cause deep hurts. However, living together as adults could be a good time to start healing those wounds and rebuilding relationships.

After having left the parental home for several years and then returning to live with her parents, one nester writes, "I have since absolved my guilty feelings of the terror I was to my parents as an adolescent. There was tremendous turmoil between myself and my parents, and between my parents themselves. Returning home brought our differences into the open. We also realized our true wishes to learn to accept each other for what we are." This family was able, during the nester period, to talk over and resolve their past difficulties. Returning home was a start in building their adult-to-adult relationship.

One mother writes that her 22-year-old daughter is kind and loving to her younger siblings, but she lacks confidence in herself. The mother attributes this to an unfortunate experience in the daughter's early years when the child's grandfather lived in his daughter's home when the grandmother was in the hospital for a prolonged period. Because the mother ran back and forth to the hospital to visit the grandmother, and then spent extra time caring for the grandfather, too much attention was taken away from the baby. The mother feels that her daughter had been shortchanged at that time, and she is dedicated to giving her all the love she can now to make up for that lost time.

Some parents are providing rehabilitation for their nesters. One mother of a 21-year-old young man working only part-time and not attending school writes, "He's trying to save money to go back to college and pay off debts incurred by trouble with the law and, we suspect, drugs. He struggled in college for two nine-month terms, but finally gave up. However, I feel that the Lord sent him back home now to us and our kinship. This is a time to rebuild his self-esteem."

One mother of a large family relates how, having her son, age 21, back home has affected their relationship. "He is able to get jobs, but gets laid off shortly after being hired. He couldn't affort to live elsewhere because he had loans to pay off, due to high risk auto insurance payments. He *says* he came back home because he couldn't afford to get an apartment, but I've since come to realize that perhaps there was a subconscious reason in returning home—to repair damaged family feelings. Our improved relationship has come about gradually, as he gained inner strength against the pressures of society." She reports that they are now better able to enjoy each other's company as adults.

"The coming home trend might just prove healthy," writes Ann, mother of nester Susanna. "It's a step forward, because in order to get along in the world, you have to get along with your parents—even if they are difficult."[5]

Some young adults nest because they need a haven.

When out of a Job. Some young people don't seem to realize the need for a sufficient, regular income as a means of supporting themselves. They come to rely upon their parents for financial support and don't seem to feel that a permanent job is really desirable or even necessary.

One mother of a 24-year-old nesting daughter lamented, "Janie is unenthusiastic about working, and is unable to support herself. She has a difficult time getting and keeping a job because she has trouble taking orders." This same mother wonders, "It seems as if some of us allow our children to live at home because we think we are helping them in time of need. Could we be doing the opposite?"

But from the nester's point of view, it can be seen very differently. One young lady on the Donahue Show complained, "I think we're putting too much emphasis on the aspect of money." Phil retorted, "What do you mean, too much emphasis? If you can't get a job, what are you going to do? We sent our children to college. They chose a major in Renaissance Literature and then they can't find a job. Now they're coming back home. I don't mean to make fun of those folks who are majoring in literature. Perhaps we could use more folks who care about the arts, letters, and culture. But the truth of the matter is, that it's a lot harder to find a job today than it was when I graduated."[6] As Donahue indicated, perhaps offspring need more guidance choosing a major in college, so that they have a marketable skill, which will bring them a living wage, after graduation. Then, perhaps college graduates will be able to support themselves and won't be forced to nest penniless in parental homes.

The following nester carried this even farther. Tammy only works part-time and can't affort an apartment. "Tammy," her mother writes, "finds work too much of an effort and boring after the first few days." She's not paying room and board, because her parents don't need it. The little money that she makes working part-time is spent on clothes and wouldn't make any difference to her parents' finances even if it was paid to them as room and board. But quite possibly it *would* make a difference in Tammy's attitude toward work if she was required to pay room and board.

Tammy's case illustrates that there is a fine line between pampering and helping a nester.

When a young person is nesting because he's out of work, he really does need a place to stay, food to eat, and, especially encouragement. His family should have love and compassion for him at this time. Occasionally when a nester is out of work, depression overcomes him and he feels that he doesn't have *any* assets! (After going the rounds of job interviews, one college graduate, with a degree in education, reported that she was almost ready to take a job in a pizza parlor.) Job responsibilities at home can help these feelings of inadequacy and depression, while the nester plays the job-waiting game. However, the nester should also receive encouragement (suggestions of job possibilities, if needed) to find meaningful work. Sometimes if too much leeway is given, the nester can become too selective in accepting a job and never really get serious about working.

When Going to School. Some nesters seem to be making a career out of going to school. They keep changing their major and so need to spend extra time in college, or they get a degree in one field after another. Meanwhile their parents are being asked to provide financial support. One mother writes, "John loves to study, and living at home has made it possible for him to advance academically. I sometimes accuse him of collecting college degrees!" Another nester is in the process of earning her third degree while she is working part-time.

There may be a fine line in the case of the permanent student, similar to the nester who isn't interested in work. Some nesters may be fearful of entering the job market and choose to find another area of study rather than join the work force. A frank discussion in either case should make this point clear. Is the nester avoiding reality by saying he wants to study yet another topic? Or does the nester really need help—financial and/or emotional—as he continues on with his studies?

When Postponing Marriage. Marriage is one of the most common reasons why offspring leave the family home. However, with weddings being put off until a later date, many young people are coming home or remaining home for longer periods of time.

In 1950, the median age for men marrying was 22.8 years, for women it was 20.3 years. However, there was no change at all between 1950 and 1960. In 1979, both sexes were waiting about two years longer. This is the *median* marrying age. That means there were as many over these ages as under. So, some even married later—much later than this chart shows. See the graph below.[7]

Table 2: Marrying Ages in the United States, 1950-1979

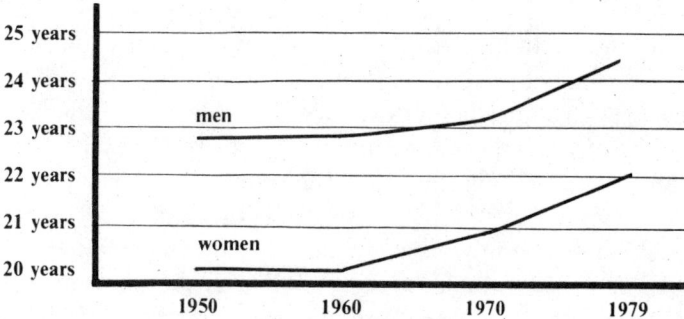

Why are young people marrying later? It could be partly because additional education and job training are now necessary to enable individuals to step into our present work force—a world that has become increasingly more technical. In one family, the father grew up on a farm home which did not have electricity until 1948. Yet, only thirty-one years later, technology had advanced so rapidly that he found it advantageous to obtain a home computer. Yes, young people do need more education now than 20-30 years ago to keep up with technology and have an employable skill. However, many young people feel that they can't afford both continued education and marriage, so they are postponing marriage until a later date. They feel that marriage is a luxury that they can't afford at present. They also fear the growing divorce rate, and want to be very, very sure that a person is the right one for them before entering into marriage.

Some young women feel that they want to be skilled in a field before they enter into marriage—just in case something goes wrong with the marriage relationship. One young woman said, "I'm going to make sure I'm always in a position to support myself and stand on my own before I enter into marriage, so that no matter what happens, I'll be all right."[8] Studies show that most married women will work outside the home for one or more decades.

Thus, parents who are concerned about a nester not marrying needn't think that their nester is the only one who is not married! Some annoyed parents feel that their daughters are just being too selective—that's why they are not getting married. And in some cases this may be true. Many young people feel that they just won't marry until "The Right One" comes along. "He will have to be my equal," one young woman says. "That means he'll have to make at least as much money as I do and should be as well educated. He'll have to understand that my job is as important to me as his is to him." This young lady hopes that her future husband likes to cook and is neat.[9] Because the social stigma against remaining single is no longer present, young people feel they can be more particular about a mate and are remaining single.

There's another reason women are remaining single: a shortage of men. It may help to ease family tensions on this point if we look at some hard facts. The Census Bureau says that between the ages of 25 and 49, women in the United

States out-number men by almost 1.2 million. One of the contributing factors of this shortage of men is the Vietnam War of the late 1960s and early 1970s. The total casualties were 155,419 individuals, mostly men, which includes 48,095 deaths.[10] (In some tribes in India and Tibet women share a husband.[11] But this is not acceptable in our country, therefore many of our young women remain single and some of them nest.)

This shortage of men is even more severe for professional women looking for a husband. These women doubled in numbers from 1970 to 1978. They want to marry a man who is their equal or superior in finances, education, and status in the community. They are finding that there just aren't enough men to go around who fulfill this criterion. As women are being educated to a greater degree, and as their earnings rise, this problem will intensify. "Meanwhile, the women who are well educated are the least married."[12]

Likewise, men's expectations of a mate are also high. "I've been told I expect too much. However, I feel if I can't have what I want, I may remain a bachelor forever," a young man said. "I'm looking for someone who is educated, intellectually mature, physically appealing, a professional person in my field or a related field, one who has a head on her shoulders, some good common sense and especially a feeling of responsibility—someone who is willing to share, to cooperate in a relationship."[13]

Some young men are looking for a companion. They place special emphasis on communication, compassion, and loyalty. "I'm looking for someone who could be my best friend," one young man wrote. "Someone I could talk to and also be willing to listen to. Someone who is outgoing, loving and loyal. I want someone who is spontaneous and will allow me to be spontaneous. Someone who will allow me to express and experience all the different emotions, including feelings of weakness. And this is a problem. A lot of women that you run into don't like their man to show any weakness. It makes them feel insecure."[14]

Some Advantages of Nesting

Some families find that nesting broadens family interests.
Life is often full, exciting, and challenging from a nester's
vantage point. When they share some of this excitement
around the dinner table or over coffee in the evening, it can
expand the parents' world. An example is a college nester
who relates news from the academic world to the parents.
One of these student nesters urged her mother to
accompany her to a class at the local university. This mom
was married at nineteen so she had not gone to college, a fact
which she often regretted. But it was frightening for her to
think of entering a large university, one with over 50,000
students, countless buildings, and many acres of land. Yet,
because of her daughter's invitation she did, and had an
opportunity to get a taste of college.

The class that mother and daughter attended together
happened to be one on public health. The day's discussion
was on the tragic situation of sudden infant death syndrome
(SIDS). (It so happened that fifteen years previously, this
family had a son who died from SIDS. The mother had
since read everything she could find on the subject and was
thus well versed on the topic.) It was a large class of 300
students, held in an amphitheater-style classroom. The
professor lectured on stage with a microphone. As he
started discussing the subject, the mother was quite able to
follow the lecture, and often whispered answers to the
professor's questions. Finally the professor asked a question
that no student was able to answer. The daughter,
suspecting that her mother knew the answer, urged her to
raise her hand. Upon recognition by the professor, she
responded with the correct reply. What an ego boost for a
40-year-old mother who had never gone to college. The
daughter, in turn, developed new respect for her mom.

As this story indicates, colleges welcome visitors who
wish to audit (listen to) classes. College nesters might even

be able to encourage their parents to register and take a few classes on their own.

Business-world nesters have jobs that, when shared with the family, can add new interest and luster to family life. One such nester was a booking agent for models. Through her job the nester met famous, interesting people and she often told her parents about them. Then too, when reading the newspaper, she told her family a little about the glamorous models protrayed in the ads. She even procurred modeling jobs for some family members, including her grandparents.

Of course, grown sons or daughters who are not living at home can also provide stimulation because of their schooling or their jobs, but it happens more easily and naturally when they are nesting. So, be open to suggestions from your grown children. Who knows what new direction your life may take.

Nesting Can Mean Shared Family Recreation. Some families complain that there is nothing that a family can do together once their children are grown. However, many families do say that their nesters join in the family fun. One mother said that her grown daughter had to be coaxed to join in family recreation because she always felt she had to study or sleep. But others say that their adult offspring often join in the family relaxation. Here's a sample of activities mentioned:

tennis	ping pong & pool
camping	cards
hunting	traveling
fishing	special events
television	visiting relatives
jigsaw puzzles	dining out

Only a few families say that their nester never or rarely joins in on family recreation.

One well-to-do family's recreational activities were reported in *Fortune* magazine. The article gave some good,

sound family relationship advice. The Hubie Clark family
was featured. This family included the father, mother, six
children and three spouses of the children. Mr. Clark
planned and paid for an elaborate family vacation, a
two-week cruise. He says, " 'If you plan an expensive enough
trip, you can get almost every family to pull together and
enjoy it. But to enjoy it with the happiness and emotional
experience that goes with such a trip is the difference. And I
do think that has happened in our family. Over the years
we've been working to understand what's important to each
member. I really think we could do the same thing around a
camping trip in the mountains and have just as much
fun.' "[15]

Unlike some executives, Clark has not sacrificed his
family for his work. "He has tried to use what he's learned
about human relations in business to strengthen the
family....While a lot of families do things together, Clark
feels that few are able to talk things out without hostility or
to resolve conflict before it hurts.... 'To be able to
understand the needs of the human beings around you and
in some ways respond is the heartbeat of a marriage and of a
family relationship,' Clark thinks. 'Our kids are beginning
to sense that.' "[16]

The Clark family is certainly a unique example. Few
families can afford a two-week cruise for eleven people.
However, any family can make recreation plans to fit their
own interests and budget. Family fun can be as elaborate as
a two-week cruise in order to work on improving family
relationships, or it can be as simple as hot, buttered popcorn
in the living room to celebrate a nester's new job.

Thus, we can see that there are many benefits that make
nesting attractive: it's more fun than living alone, it's
cheaper, it allows many nesters to save money, it's a way for
families to get to know each other as adults, it offers
companionship, it broadens family interests, it's an
opportunity to mend damaged relationships, it's a haven in
time of need, and it's also enjoyable to share family fun

together. No wonder almost sixteen million American adult sons and daughters are nesting.

Problems Relating to Nesters

Young people are drawn to return to, or remain in, the parental home for various reasons mentioned previously. However, the consequences of nesting can often be a host of problems—both large and small. Life with an adult offspring can raise specific problems that are unique to nesting. Some young people forget the need to be considerate to other family members. Then irritations blossom and misunderstandings can arise. In addition, nesting can cause stress on the parental marriage bond. It's sometimes difficult to have various age groups living in one house. The atmosphere can get overheated, and relationships can get strained and tense. We all want to live orderly, predictable, calm lives, but life with a nester oftentimes is the very opposite. It's an added burden to have adult children living at home, especially if that person's life is in turmoil—which is frequently the case with a nester.

If we analyze the problems and then think and talk about them, we will find that generally there is a workable solution. By looking at other families and how they cope with conflicts, we can learn how to overcome these problems. Vicky, a mother of fifteen children, seven children born to her and her husband and eight adopted, comments, "Sometimes I feel that other people think it doesn't take much intelligence to run a family. On the contrary, it takes a brilliant person to do this, because of the multiplicity of problems that arise. I had a profession previous to marriage, so I know a profession has its own headaches, its own discipline. But that profession wasn't nearly as taxing as being a homemaker. I know that the grass isn't greener on the other side of the fence. I've been there. Sure, it's work being a parent, but anything worthwhile requires time and effort."[17]

The Need to be Considerate. In an extended family
household, a lack of privacy and freedom can be just as
binding for the nesters as for the other family members. A
nester's peers who live independently experience a
self-concern that a nester doesn't share. Instead, the nester
has to learn to be considerate, to cooperate and to respect
others' rights in various areas. Problems to be aware of are:

*Space and Territory:
  —Leaving clothes, dirty dishes, or books scattered throughout
    the home
  —Being aware that certain areas of the home may be private
    domain (bedrooms, closets, etc.)

*Time:
  —Insisting that everyone help find a lost item
  —Sharing bathroom time
  —Asking someone else to mend a piece of clothing at the last
    minute or prepare a quick meal when one is late for work
  —Insisting, "I need help right *now!*"
  —Being on the telephone too long

*Possessions:
  —Borrowing clothes
  —Borrowing a car
  —"Borrowing" food for a party

*Sound:
  —Disrupting volume of radio or stereo
  —Receiving telephone calls late at night

As an example of one of the above, we can look at a
family where a daughter in her mid-20's returned home. She
had no car of her own so, in order to get to work, she was
allowed to use her mother's car. One day, the carless mother
desperately needed groceries, and had to use a bicycle to get
to the store. Pushing a bicycle heavily laden with groceries
up a steep hill was not her favorite pastime—not at all what
she had envisioned herself doing when she reached her 50th
birthday. Still this mother, out of consideration for her
daughter, was willing to make the sacrifice of her car.
Sometimes we have to put aside our own personal wants,
feelings, and needs because there are other people in the
house to be considered.

Small irritations can grow. It isn't usually the big things that cause irritations in living with a nester—it's often the little things. In this respect, nesting is very similar to the marriage relationship. One mother was quite irritated that her 21-year-old daughter frequently forgot to turn off the curling iron that she used for her hair. She also sometimes went to work leaving behind a red-hot iron that she had used to press her clothes. This daughter always left home looking neat, clean, and beautiful which required a great deal of time. But turning off small appliances didn't seem to be on

Parents often nag about late hours or messy rooms. But how much do any of us change after we become adults?

her mind as she prepared to leave the home. This happened frequently despite all her mother's efforts to remind her daughter. It got to be such a common occurrence that the mother automatically checked these two items each morning after her daughter left for work. This irritated the mother and she found herself becoming increasingly resentful.

So, one morning this mother decided to phone the utility company and find out just how much it would cost if either of these two items were left on for twenty-four hours—the length of time they would be left on until her daughter used them again. Much to her amazement, mother found out that it only cost six cents to run the curling iron for twenty-four hours. However, the pressing iron was a different story—ninety-four cents for the same time period. On the basis of that information, mother decided it was inconsequential to worry about the curling iron, as long as it wasn't left on a towel or any place where it could be a fire hazard. Instead, she concentrated on the pressing iron, and relayed this financial information to her daughter. Thereafter, she found a decided improvement over the earlier frequency of both left-on appliances.

This mother has learned to concentrate on an important area and ignore a trivial one. She related that she found herself thinking, "What was I worrying about an insignificant six cents for? As long as she leaves it in a safe place, that curling iron isn't worth making a fuss about!" Lesson learned: the reaction to a problem should be in proportion to the severity of the problem itself.

Not only do parents, brothers and sisters of nesters experience irritations, but so do the nesters themselves while they are living at home. One 22-year-old full-time college student who is working part-time in the accounting department of a large hotel, related that he is happy to be living at home and that there is very little friction in the home. However, he continued, his mother complains about his spelling and this bothers him. In reading through his questionnaire answers, it soon became evident why his mother was complaining. He had an innovative approach to spelling; "iceolated" and "obinion." His mother was probably trying to make him aware of this problem, but does nagging about it help her son? Possibly mother may be better off to relieve pressure on this point, as her son is well aware of this academic deficiency by now. It's so easy for parents to fall into a habit of nagging their nesters. Young people complain that parents nag about late hours, messy rooms, style of dress, table manners, and the way they drive the car. Most parents believe it's for their nesters' own good. But how much will, or can, these nesters change now that they are adults?

Humor columnist Erma Bombeck writes about annoyances caused by nesters. She says that when all her children grew up and moved out, she treated herself to a celery green carpet in the spare bedroom. She writes, "Three months later, one of my children moved back with, among other things, a set of drums that leaked oil. My celery green carpet looked like a left-over. When he left we had it cleaned and began again. The next prodigal son brought a dog that had a sofa wish, a car that was not garage trained and leaked oil when it was parked there and used towels like they were disposable nose tissues that popped up automatically in a box. The next one to return let me use my own phone, but kept hours like a fireman."[18] As Bombeck illustrates, looking for and seeing the humor in a situation helps us to live with annoyances and small irritations.

In addition to annoying habits of nesters, parents may have to learn how to cope with an unexpected crisis. A mother of two nesting sons felt that once she had adjusted herself to seeing her sons fixing carburetors on the kitchen table, she'd be able to face up to anything else they'd do. However, her resolve was definitely tested when the following incident occurred. One Saturday she had cleaned the house spotless in preparation for Sunday dinner guests. The next morning she went to church and returned home to find that two freshly painted shock absorbers were baking in the oven which she needed in order to cook dinner.[19]

It is sometimes difficult living with blood relations, but living with in-law's can be even harder. Careful consideration should be given ahead of time before living together is even attempted. Married nesters can create unique problems. One mother suggested her daughter and son-in-law move in with her because they were having trouble saving money for a down payment on a home of their own. But very quickly problems arose. Mother and son-in-law were not getting along at all! Finally, after six months the mother told her daughter, "Either he goes, or you both go." Her daughter stayed, but the husband left.[20]

Misunderstandings. Underlying misunderstandings can cause havoc in family relationships. One father, Jack, blew up in anger one Saturday at his 21-year-old daughter, Corky, for not helping with family cleaning chores. She lashed back, "Well, I pay rent, but no one bothered to tell me last week that the rust remover on the water system wasn't working. I washed my clothes and three blouses were ruined." Believing this was off the subject, Jack didn't want to listen and walked away from her. At lunchtime, she was too upset to eat. After thinking that Corky would probably be angry at him for a week and seeing that his wife was distraught over the two of them fighting, Jack decided to call a truce. They talked it out, working out both the problem of the chores and the water softener, and the whole family had lunch together peacefully.

Corky and her father really have a misunderstanding, though, about room and board. Corky thinks that the $15 a week she pays is enough, but her father disagrees. Given this disagreement, there will probably be another fight tomorrow or next week. It would be so much better if Jack and Corky could talk over their differences of opinion about room and board than to ignore this underlying problem. Corky's position is that $15 is a lot to pay for room and board since she is usually on a diet and doesn't eat that much anyway. She also believes her parents would have to heat her bedroom whether she or her sister slept in it. And besides, her parents know that she only makes $740 a month! On the other hand, Jack realizes it would probably cost his daughter $150 a month for apartment rental (if she shared it with a friend), groceries would be at least an additional $50, and other items like utilities, toiletries, and laundry would easily cost Corky double or triple what she now pays for room and board. Also, if Corky did have an apartment, she would still have to do the same cleaning chores she was balking at in her parents' home. So, what Jack and Corky really need is to discuss their various viewpoints, let each other see where they are coming from, and set a compromise price for room and board.

Communication Gaps. In Chapter 5 the problem of communicating will be dealt with in depth, but here it will be briefly noted that problems in communicating can be some of the consequences of nesting. The method of communication that families followed throughout the growing-up years are no longer applicable after the offspring are grown. Parents can't issue orders to their adult offspring in the same manner they did to the children when they were young—and expect to be automatically obeyed. Nesters are now adults and make more of their own decisions. This does not mean that house rules need not apply to the nester. But it does mean that families have to discover new ways of relating to one another, of realizing what is expected of both parents and nesters. When expectations are unclear, misunderstandings and hurt feelings are inevitable. "I am forever biting my tongue," one mother with a nesting son writes. Maybe what she didn't realize was that, as one adult to another adult, there needs to be a clarification of expectations, perhaps a modification of rules, to fit the needs of both parents and nesters. There obviously will be a period of adjustment after the nester reaches adulthood, but as one mother said, "If all parties involved feel very positively about the idea of living together, I do think it can work."

Stress on the Parental Marriage Bond. A problem that is often unspoken with grown children living in the family home is a lessening of the intimacy between parents, as they struggle to fit another adult into their daily lives.

Dealing with problems relating to their nester can sometimes cause serious difficulties between parents. One author writes that an extended family household creates a radically different set of emotional arrangements, with a strong likelihood of a considerably diluted relationship between spouses.[21] For example, one spouse may feel differently about a topic, such as room and board, than the other spouse. Also, there may be friction between a parent and a nester which is so draining that there isn't much emotional intensity left over for the spouse. These problems should be talked out, with everyone realizing that they are transitory. Eventually the nester will move out and the tensions between parents will ease. Once again they'll be alone together with lots of time for just themselves.

On the other hand, when there are problems between the spouses, the nester may try to solve these problems. One nester wrote that he had a tendency to play "marriage counselor" for his parents. He thought he was intruding with great wisdom about how his parents should treat one another. That didn't work, he reported, because whenever he tried, it usually ended in both parents being hostile toward him.

In another family, the marriage had deteriorated, and the wife was decidedly bored. So she concentrated her attention on her only child, a nesting son. He and his friends, one of whom had also moved in with them, provided most of her conversation and companionship. Meanwhile, she had little communication with her husband. When they did talk, they avoided personal issues and topics that touched on feelings and opinions. He left early in the morning to go to work, and when he came home around 6:00, the family immediately ate supper. After that, the husband watched television and then went to bed. Without the conversation and companionship of her son and his friends, in whose lives she became deeply interested, she wouldn't be getting her emotional needs fulfilled. But what will happen when the nester eventually leaves home?

Conclusion

We can see that nesters are drawn to living at home for various reasons and needs, and that parents can gain a great deal from the situation as well. It's beneficial to concentrate on the happy aspects and advantages of nesting, for then life looks rosier. If there is a tendency for a problem to arise, and everyone is aware of this tendency, the family is less likely to let that problem keep recurring. But problems resulting in life with a nester need to be faced and resolved, or else these problems can multiply. There are certain irritating habits of nesters and certain inflexibilities of parents, that may need to change. Once a family is aware of problems, they can discuss them and try to solve them. There's no hope of solving a problem unless everyone is aware a problem exists.

"In the parent's mind, a child grows, but does not age."
—Columnist Sydney Harris[1]

CHAPTER IV

Independence/Maturity

Everyone, it seems, is worried about the long-term effects of nesting. Psychologists and sociologists are concerned that nesters will stagnate by living at home. Some parents worry that they may be clinging to their kids and hindering their growth. Other parents worry that they are pushing their kids out of the nest too soon.

No matter what we're worried about, there are important questions we need to ask ourselves. Will our nester become an independent and mature adult while living at home, or is it necessary for him to move out in order to grow? Many of us ask ourselves if nesting will have a positive or negative long-range effect on our kids. We ask the question, but we're just not sure of the answer. That's because the answer is different for all of us.

Independence and Maturity/
Dependence and Immaturity

Nesters want to be independent, and parents want their kids to become independent. But what does this mean? *Webster's Dictionary* offers one view.

in-de-pen-dence: not subject to the control of another, able to act
on one's own authority, not having to rely on another person or
thing, a person unwilling to be subject to or under obligation to
another, resenting control, shunning advice, uninfluenced by any
other person or thing, standing by oneself, not dependent on
another for support, either possessing or earning means of support.

In addition, *Roget's Thesaurus* also offers a few insights
into what independence means: self-governing, free,
self-reliant, disconnected, separate, self-sufficient. So, with
these definitions, we can see a little more clearly what being
independent means.

Then there's the subject of maturity. The dictionary
defines maturity as "brought by natural process to
completeness of growth and development; full-grown; ripe
or pertaining to a condition of full development." The
thesaurus uses the synonyms "ripe," "complete," and
"adult." Psychoanalyst Anna Freud defines being mature as
"to have the capacity to work and to love."[2] It's clear that
our nesters need to be independent, and that they also need
to become mature, emotionally stable, and sensitive.

How can we tell whether our nester is moving in the right
direction, or whether he is remaining dependent and
immature? The dictionary defines dependence as: "a state of
being supported by others, living at the expense of others,
governed by, rely on, contingent on, conditioned by or
connected with others." Immature means: "not arrived at
full development, unripe, unfinished, youthful, not yet
mature." The thesaurus tells us that other meanings for
immature are: "half-grown, unripe, green, undeveloped,
raw, callow, young and unready."

Types of Nesters

With the above definitions it will be easier to assess
whether a nester is independent, responsible, and mature. In
order for adult offspring to become truly independent, they
must find their own identity—a realistic image of themselves.

In finding their own identity, our offspring fall into four different categories:[3]

1. **Foreclosures:** these offspring commit themselves to their parents' views without question. This type tends to live at home for longer periods than the other types.

2. **Diffusers:** these offspring seem aimless, having no set vocation or ideological direction. They never really had a home in the first place, and they talk of feeling abandoned.

3. **Moratoriers:** these offspring remain uncertain about their own identity. They are always in the process of leaving, symbolically packing their bags, full of questioning doubts about their own identity.

4. **Achievers:** these offspring question the views of their parents, go through a crisis and find a self-chosen career goal and ideology. They have grown up by having gone through a period of questioning. Their values may perhaps be the same as their parents but at least they've gone through a stretch of experimenting with alternatives.[4]

If we can pinpoint what category our own nesters fall into, we may be able to understand, guide, and help our nesters on their road to independence.

Types of Parents

In understanding nesters it is important to examine types of parents that formed the nesters. In identifying with one or more of these parent types it will be possible to have a better perspective when relating with nesters.

The Authoritarian Parent. The authoritarian parent has a tendency to see his children, regardless of age, as his property, the way he regards an automobile or a television set as his property. He orders his children's behavior as he would any other object over which he wishes to have control. If the parent is the authoritarian type, there's bound to be trouble when the child reaches adulthood! An authoritarian parent issues directives and expects them to be obeyed. When his child was young, this parent was able to dictate an order and the child was compelled to obey.

However, when that child reaches adulthood, this is no longer effective. At this stage of the game, the nester usually feels he does not have to obey a parental order. He no longer will continue to play the role of a subservient robot. Some parents maintain, even after the child is an adult, that, "As long as he is under my roof, what I say goes!" A nester who blindly carries out an order is not learning to be independent. Is this blind obedience really what the parent wants?

The extreme authoritarian parent will drive a wedge between himself and his children. Let's look at Mr. Smith. He issued orders to his five children and expected instant, exact obedience. For instance, when the boys were told to wash the family car, they were allotted only two buckets of water, told to use both sides of the sponge, and wipe in a horizontal direction. As the boys grew up, they began to rebel, and as soon as they were able, they left the family home and severed all communications with their father. These children still come home to visit — but only with their mother and only when they know that their father will not be home.

Another example of a parent who is too authoritarian is one who still insists on ordering each detail of his grown offspring's life. For instance, he insists that he knows what type of car or suit his son should buy — and where to buy it.

The Permissive Parent. On the other hand, being permissive can spell trouble too, because this parent views ownership as a family affair. The child of permissive parents is allowed full use of all the family belongings. However, when that child becomes an adult, the system is no longer effective because he "requires" the family car, the brother's new shirt, mother's free time. ("But you aren't doing anything, Mom, so can't you fix my jeans? I have to leave in seven minutes, and I really want to wear them!") This nester often will expect tuition paid to the college of his choice or free room and board even though he has a good-paying job.

All too often the nester of a permissive parent will use the family car without permission and without refilling the gas tank, because he feels that it belongs to the family and he is part of the family. Many nesters of permissive parents have a difficult time learning responsible use of their parents' goods and time.

Parents who are either strongly permissive or authoritarian may need to find new ways of communicating once their children become grown up. Authoritarian parents may need a new awareness that their children are now adults and must begin to make their own decisions. Permissive parents may need a new awareness that their children are now adults and must begin to supply their own needs.

Neither the authoritarian nor the permissive parent is helping the child grow to be an independent person. But worse than the authoritarian parents or permissive parents is a mix, one of each! The permissive parent feels that the other parent is too hard or tough on the "children" even though they really are adults. ("You'll drive the children away from us and the house.") The authoritarian parent feels that the other parent is coddling the children. ("They'll never grow up if you keep giving them everything that they ever need or even want.") There is disagreement between the parents on how to relate to the children. This difference of opinion ripples throughout the family and is felt by everyone.

Some families may not identify with the above types of parents. If so, they may be able to relate to the middle-of-the-road parent. This type of parent will allow his offspring to choose a household job from among many, with a time deadline for completion of the task. Another example of a middle-of-the-road parent is one who has a curfew with a known punishment for any violation.

Gradual Steps Toward Independence

Slowly the offspring begins to take control of his life, first making small decisions, then later larger ones. It's a gradual process.

Many offspring take quite a long time to actually become independent. They do it in steps — a visit to a cousin's home, a vacation, time living on campus at school, traveling, or apartment living for various time spans. Generally, each time they leave it's for a longer period. But they do keep returning. When the break is finally made, the step is hardly noticed, since it was so gradual.

Psychologist Arthur Maslow also suggests that leave-taking doesn't have to be done in one big leap—it can be a gradual progression. He feels that telephoning, visiting back and forth, dropping in to use the washing machine, and even accepting furniture from the folks' basement, makes the separation easier.[5]

Psychologist Howard Halpern explains it this way. "Development is not a straight line....A step backward may follow two steps forward. You may have to take the wrong step in order to know the right step. You may discover after you move out that leaving was premature and that you need to return home for a while. Or some offspring may stay at home, but realize that they can't be happy or adult as long as they do remain at home. All our trials and errors help us to work out the balance of closeness and distance that will work for us."[6]

Another writer, Grace Weinstein, describes it as a seesaw—going up and down, back and forth between the security that one receives from her parents and the independence that she can have on her own. The parents teeter-totter also between holding on to their offspring and letting go.[7] Some days the seesaw dips one way, other days it drifts in the opposite direction.

Growing up and forming our own identity is a process or a series of steps that one takes. It's never quite done or

One of life's greatest joys is to know and respect your children on an adult-to-adult basis.

complete. Hopefully, we'll continue to grow, learn and change all through our life. Sometimes it's a struggle — somewhat like a chick breaking its way out of its eggshell: a little peck here and a bigger peck there. It's painful oftentimes, but satisfying and challenging too, when we can see growth and progress in ourselves. For many offspring it's a real struggle to break away, physically and emotionally, because they feel tied to their parents who loved, protected, and guided them from infancy onward. It's hard to cut the cord.

Parents and offspring should be alert to the fact that the time of leave-taking is often fraught with conflict. One mother reported that the summer before her daughter left for her freshman year at college was the first time they had ever had any real disagreements. A study done with 142 Yale freshmen showed that anxiety and anger often accompanied an artificial deadline for leaving home. The study showed that anger served as a separating function. It's easier for a nester to leave home if he is angry. "The stronger the fear of not being able to sever the umbilical cord, the greater the intensity of anger before leaving." Female emotions in this area were more intense than those of males. Anxiety and aggression toward the parents seemed to be a normal part of the transition of leaving home and becoming independent.[8] The offspring is pulling away, yearning to find an autonomous identity, but feeling, very powerfully, the dependence he's always had on his parents. The parents want to protect and hold onto their offspring, yet they know that they must let go. It's a push and pull situation, according to Psychiatrist Daniel Goleman.[9]

"Did you pack the independence, Mom?"
(It's harder for some to become independent.)

It's definitely harder for some offspring to travel the road toward independence than for others. In this case, an artificial deadline may help — such as college entrance or turning 18 years of age — as long as it's not strictly enforced. After all, independence and maturity don't jump into their suitcase as the youngster closes the front door! When the deadline arrives however, some offspring may not be ready to leave. And if they're pushed out anyway it can be devastating for them.

Suzie, a young adult in her early twenties who appeared on the Phil Donahue Show, said, "My father is a strong believer in the idea that when one of his kids turns 18, (that child) moves out. So I moved out at 18, but I couldn't support myself. So, I got married and had a baby. Then I got divorced. After that it was even worse — I was a single parent! So, I got married again and had another baby. Now I have two children, who I hope will grow up perfectly independent, but I would never, never tell them they're not welcome at home. If any time they wanted to come home, they're always welcome." Phil questioned her, "You got married because you were thrown out?" Suzie responded, "Oh, I don't want to blame my father, okay?" But Phil continued, "But it certainly did encourage you to hook up?" Affirmative reply. Phil then commented that he felt "there are far too many marriages that are formed in order to get out of the house — far too many marriages formed out of lack of parental support."[10] So it may be wise to think twice before setting an arbitrary deadline for departure.

"With no clear social norm, how can parents know whether they are clinging too long to their children, or erring in the opposite direction, pushing them out the door too soon?" Daniel Goleman asks in *Psychology Today*. He then goes on to refer to some research work done by others. Frederick Coons, a former director of the psychological counseling service at the University of Indiana, says it's harder for girls, only children, and youngest children to leave home. However, variations from individual to individual may be enormous and for many young people, the passage actually is far smoother than psychologists ever envisioned. Success or failure in the venture may depend as much on the parents' feelings about their own lives as on the resources of the young people themselves.[11] Are the parents able to allow the offspring to leave without objections? Do the parents have full lives on their own without needing the presence of their children? Are the offspring prepared to face the world apart from the parents?

One mother of nine children writes, "I firmly believe a child at 18 is not an adult and ready to live in the outside world today. He may think he is, but in reality, he isn't. A gradual weaning away from home, parents, and family is necessary. When they do strike out on their own and 'fail' to make it because it's premature, they come back home for that needed security, confidence building, growing up, maturing time. Most importantly, they need to know they are still loved and accepted. Failing at something takes much confidence from them, and inadvertently, they come back home to regroup. Most often they don't realize why they are coming home. On the surface it's finances, but it usually is much deeper than that. I realize some teens are more ready at 18 than others, but most aren't mature at that age."

It is interesting to note, though, that a 1976 study by the American Council of Life Insurance showed that kids with only a high school diploma (as compared to a college degree), young married couples, and those from a lower-income background are more likely to be self-sufficient and to seek a second job in times of need. College graduates, singles, and those from more affluent backgrounds are more inclined to turn to, and rely upon, their parents for help.[12] This may be because lower income families are not *able* to give financial help and so the kids don't expect it.

The philosophy of weaning a baby from the breast can very easily be applied to adult nesters. La Leche League, an organization devoted to teaching good mothering through breastfeeding, holds this philosophy toward weaning: "Don't offer, but don't refuse." That is, if the mother feels it is time that the baby weans, she shouldn't offer the breast, but if the baby indicates he wants to nurse, she shouldn't refuse. It's a painless, natural, and pleasant method of weaning. And weaning does eventually occur, when the baby is ready.

Like these weaning mothers, we don't want to keep our offspring dependent on us beyond what is good for them. But we also don't want to refuse to help them. So, if a family is able to accommodate an adult offspring, La Leche League's slogan of "don't offer, but don't refuse" may be a good guide.

"Parents sometimes have a peculiar way of telescoping time," write Comer and Quinby in *Mademoiselle* magazine, "despite the fact that you are obviously old enough to be making your own decisions, your parents may still occasionally become tangled in their memories of you as a child and want to keep helping you." It's really difficult for many parents to make the transition of seeing their offspring change from a child to an adult.[13]

A possible reason for this difficulty may be that families are set up for dependency. After all, the primary function of the family is to care for children. It's difficult for parents to change their frame of reference and view their children as adults just because they have turned 18. Even when the transition is made, the situation can still be very trying. Parents see a living, breathing adult in front of them, but then many wonder why this offspring isn't in the outside world taking care of himself, like other adults they know. It's just as hard for some offspring because they have been dependent upon their parents for 18 years. It can be very difficult for some of them to make the transition from dependence to independence.

In order to get a better idea of independence/dependence, take this little quiz just for fun. Check the degrees of maturity possessed by the individuals described below. Read the quiz and then choose a number from one to ten which denotes the degree of maturity you feel the young person possesses. Number one denotes extreme dependency, number two less dependency, and on up to number ten which denotes complete independency.

Quiz

— **A.** Nester helps out with expenses when he's working, frequently sleeps late after he's been out having a few beers with his friends the night before. Doesn't get along with other family members, nor help with any chores around the house.

— **B.** Offspring lives away from home, has a good job, car, and apartment, but keeps such a messy place that he has to wade through the mess. Offspring always washes his clothes at his parents' place.

— **C.** Nester contributes part of income to household, helps with daily chores such as cleaning, cooking and laundry. Offspring requires five calls from someone to get up in the morning.

— **D.** Offspring lives away from home, sharing a clean apartment with a friend. Both have good jobs and cars. They fulfill all their own daily needs. But they spend every free moment they have with their family.

— **E.** Nester has a job, his own car and insurance, helps around the house, pays room and board to his parents, and gets along well with other family members. Offspring asks parents for advice but makes own decisions.

"A" shouts dependency by not paying his way at home, sleeping late, not getting along with family members, nor helping with household chores, and thus should be graded as a "1." "B" shows independency in being able to support himself in his own apartment with a good job and car, but shows immaturity in letting his apartment get dirty and needing to use his parents' laundry facilities, and so merits a "7." "C" indicates independency in contributing income and helping with chores, but shows dependency in needing to have five calls to get up in the morning, and consequently is given a "9." "D" portrays independence in apartment living, job and transportation, but shows some dependence on his family for needing to spend so much time with them, also resulting in a "9." "E" is certainly an independent, mature person, even though he lives at home, and is therefore awarded a "10."

Your grading decisions may differ from the above, but reading the quiz and making a decision regarding maturity, may have been helpful in seeing varying degrees of maturity in nesters.

Adult offspring may view themselves as independent when they move out of the parental home. Are they really independent, though, if they continue to rely on parents for money, emotional support, or other daily needs like food and laundry? On the other hand, is it necessarily true that an adult offspring living at home is dependent, especially if he is fulfilling all the characteristics of an independent person?

Nesters are in transition from dependence to independence. Transitions are hard for all of us. Some offspring have a more difficult time accomplishing this feat. Parents need patience at this time. However, if parents think about it, they will probably recall that the transition from youth to adulthood was one of *their* most difficult times of transition.

Parents can help nesters become independent.

To aid in this transition, there are some concrete things that parents can think about and do.

See your nesters as adults. Parents need to view their nesters as adults, as capable and responsible individuals. Even if they aren't, if you act like they are, it might come true —they may develop into independent, mature persons.

Assuredly, it's difficult for a parent to see his child as an adult. Syndicated columnist Sydney Harris tells why this is so. He feels he can't be rational about the fact that his children have grown up because he loves his children, and how can love be rational? Here's Harris' column on the subject:

> Are parents rational about their children? No. Parents aren't rational because love isn't rational. Young people can recognize this about romantic love, but they find it hard to accept the same fierce element in parental affection.
>
> What brings this up was my eldest daughter's question the other day. "Let me ask you something, Dad," she began, in a tone of patiently controlled exasperation that every experienced parent is familiar with.
>
> "I sailed around the Mediterranean in a schooner when I was 17," she recited slowly and carefully. "I hiked through the Pyrenees from Spain to Paris. I've done rock climbing and deep-sea diving and slept in rain forests in the jungle of Indonesia. Right?"
>
> "Right," I said, shivering at this recital, as a man would who gets hysterical while taking a shower if a bit of soap stings his eye. "So what?"
>
> "So this," she went on. "When I'm home, and I'm going to the corner drugstore to pick up a shampoo, why do you always tell me to be careful how I cross the street?"
>
> There is no satisfactory answer a parent can give to this.
>
> All I could mumble in response was that when I was a man of 50, my mother would lean out of the window when I left and remind me not to drive too fast. If I were 80, and she were still alive, I would be getting the same admonition. No matter the age, a child is a child.
>
> There is another factor, too, that children find it hard to understand. When they are far away, there is nothing we can do about their safety or welfare. They are in the hands of the gods. Parents try not to think about it, hoping that by blotting it out, the fateful call or cable will never come.
>
> But when they are close by again, the old protective urge quickly reasserts itself, and it matters not how far they have been or how long gone, or even how well they have demonstrated their survival ability.
>
> Most accidents, after all, happen around the corner, not in the rain forest. Man is a more dangerous foe to man than the elements of nature or animals in the wild. The most instinctive act of nearly every creature is to protect its young, and with humans this response persists a lifetime.
>
> In the parents mind, a child grows, but does not age. Rational? No. But if we were wholly rational, would we want children at all?[14]

Harris feels that if a child lives away from home and is out of sight, his parents don't worry about him. When the child comes back to roost, though, his parents may once again become concerned, and start giving unsolicited advice.

Married couples who are nesters complain of having to be answerable to parental authority, even though they have reached adulthood years before. One couple says they are having severe problems with the wife's father (with whom they are living) because he insists upon waiting up until they come home at night. "My dad just won't go to sleep until he hears us at the door," explained the wife/daughter. "According to my parents, we never really grew up," she says.[15]

So, we can see how sometimes it is difficult for nesters to be considered adults by their parents. What a handicap for the nester in his growth toward independence. But what a challenge for both nester and parents to make it happen!

Don't insist on giving. To untie the apron strings is particularly difficult for children whose parents insist on giving. Giving can come in many forms: money, cars, free room and board, or words of wisdom. By giving nesters too many material goods, parents can make them think that these things come easy in the real world. This, of course, is not true! Thus parents are misleading their offspring. It's very tempting for nesters to accept a gift, but the young adult has to take responsibility for not being seduced, especially if the parent is easily hurt by non-acceptance of the gift. It's not always a simple matter for an offspring to say, "Thanks, but no thanks."[16]

Howard Halpern, a psychologist and popular author, gives us a further insight, "Every parent has two parts, an inner child and a mature parent. The mature parenting part really wants to launch the child and when that part is dominant, gifts can be given with no strings attached. But the inner child part of the parent may need to cling, fearing abandonment by the offspring and if that part of the parent is dominant, a gift may be intended to control." He states that some parents unconsciously want to keep their grown children dependent and close to them.[17] In a way, they attempt to bribe their children into staying with them, or at least into being dependent on them. So, if you want to help your children on the road to independence, you may want to analyze your gift-giving patterns.

Release your authority. Parents must realize that their task of child rearing is finished when their offspring reaches adulthood. Dr. Roberta Chaplan, a New York psychologist, says that a young, dependent child should accept authority from the parent, but that an adult should ultimately become his own authority.[18] For example, when a child was small, he did what he was told by his parents, but now that he is an adult, he makes his own decisions and takes responsibility for those decisions.

The following poem, written decades ago, encourages a mother to release her hold over her grown son.

To the Mother of a Young Son

Hold your breath but not his hand
When he climbs to the top of the tree.
You can't go, too — the journey's his.
There's a lot of world to see.
He found a haven in your arms,
But now he's on his own,
The track is there and he must run.
And he must run alone.
The cord was cut when you gave him birth
They placed him near your heart.
Yours to guide, yours to love
And yours to watch depart.[19]

—Shirley Taylor Lambert

A nester is an adult in the process of becoming his own authority on concerns in his life. Nesters expecially don't want to be subservient to another after reaching adulthood. So, parents need to let go of the strings and release their authority. In other words, there has to be a shift for the parent from the authority figure to an equal adult. This is a freeing action, in and of itself. It releases your adult offspring and enables him to grow. Parents can still pass on their experience after their children become adults. But now they must share it as loving teachers, and no longer as authority figures.[20]

Keep your advice to yourself. Parental advice: keep it, unless you're asked for it. While maintaining a real interest in our nesters' lives, parents have to resist the temptation to try to manage our grown children's lives. Some parents have a difficult time relinquishing their role as advice givers, but it's important to learn to give advice without coercing, to disagree without provoking guilt, and to allow freedom, while at the same time pointing out dangers and pitfalls.[21]

One nester complains that her parents are still trying to run her life. But what she doesn't seem to realize is that she continues to discuss every aspect of her life with them. By giving her parents so many details, she is implying that she really wants their advice.[22] A nester needs to realize that if he takes responsibility for his own actions, his parents can relax and often will allow the nester to take care of himself. If the offspring isn't taking responsibility, it's time for a good family discussion.

Jory Graham, whose syndicated newspaper column "Time for Living" deals with cancer patients, wrote an article which was especially applicable to this topic of how parents and families can help nesters become independent. Graham wrote that the help that is needed by cancer patients is the kind that encourages efforts to become independent. They need this encouragement just as much as they need to be listened to quietly as they share some of their deepest feelings. She could just as easily have been voicing the thoughts of adult offspring struggling to become independent. "Each time you (parents) usurp our fundamental right to make our own decisions and our own mistakes, you become more of a problem to us than a help. That's when we become resentful and unappreciative. If the time comes that we need help, we'll let you know."[23] How beautifully spoken. This is independence.

Parents must learn when to help and when to let the kids help themselves. That's not easy for parents, but that's what is needed. A study[24] done by a national research firm (Yankelovich, Skelly and White), shows that younger parents are rather self-oriented, while older, more traditional parents are likely to sacrifice for their children. So, older, traditional parents must be especially alert to this tendency to do things for their offspring. It will be harder for these parents to allow their offspring to become independent. Maybe a few sample questions will help you analyze whether your nester really wants advice or help from you. When your nester tells you about a problem you can ask: "Can you handle this yourself? Do you want some advice on how to solve it? Do you need help solving it? Or do you just want me to listen?"

In this way you're shifting the responsibility and the decision-making to your nester. You can also determine whether your nester wants to dump the problem on you (which you could transfer back to him), or whether he only needs advice or help in solving the problem.

Erma Bombeck, in a column entitled, "Kids grow up only when their parents permit it,"[25] lets us see the humor of our kids becoming independent. Erma writes that parents say, "You have to learn to live with your own mistakes." Yet, in the next breath we find ourselves saying things like, "Look, Daddy and I will pay to have your car repaired and you can pay us back later." Another example she used was a mother saying, "It's time you were responsible for yourself." But then adding, "I've made a dental appointment for you Tuesday and picked up your cleaning."

If we want our nester to act maturely, we can't keep treating him like a child. We need to remember that it helps our nester to act in a mature manner if we see him as an adult.

Ways that nesters can show maturity and be independent

Nesters have many ways to show that they are independent.

Make decisions and take the responsibility for them. One of the criteria of independence is being able to make decisions, and feel confident about those decisions, without having to seek approval. If a nester is able to look at a problem from all angles, weigh the consequences of a decision, and then go ahead and decide, fully accepting all the consequences, he is certainly fulfilling one of the criteria of being an independent person. A person cannot feel really independent unless he is comfortable with the decisions he makes.

One mother of two nesters, a son, age 21, and a daughter, age 20, says that she encourages her nesters to solve their own problems and make their own decisions. She relates this story. When her daughter needed to get the brakes repaired on her car, she decided herself where to take it for repair. This meant finding out the various places or people who fixed brakes and then determining where she could get the best quality of work for the least amount of money. By solving this problem, she was able to grow more toward being independent.

Pay your way. One parent on the Phil Donahue Show felt that it is necessary for a nester to pay his own way, especially rent and utilities, thereby proving to the world that he is independent.[26] To be considered independent in our society, where one can't get along without money, means paying what it costs to house, feed, clothe, insure, transport, entertain, and clean you. The list could go on and on. The nester's budget will tell him how much he can spend in each area.

Take care of your daily needs. One parent, a mother of three nesters (ages 25, 20 and 18), said that she felt that accepting and assuming the responsibilities of life was a real sign of independence. She felt that if an individual were able to care for himself and his own daily needs, he would be well on the road to being a self-sufficient person. And this includes a lot of daily, routine things that sometimes elude us, such as:

- keeping living space clean
- washing clothes
- ironing clothes
- mending clothes
- balancing checkbook
- preparing income tax materials
- filing important papers
- planning a budget
- planning menus
- buying food
- preparing food
- washing dishes
- typing papers
- taking care of car or bike
- undertaking repair jobs
- getting to work on time

   This is not to say that all people should be able to do all these things on their own, with their own power. The point is, all people should be able to take care of them or decide who can help them with the things that they can't do. These tasks don't happen unless someone does them.

Be stable emotionally. Emotional stability is a good sign of a mature, independent person, and is especially important in the relationships we have with family and friends. When relating to family members, a mature nester treats them with care, concern, and respect. If he doesn't, and if the nester tends to treat friends better than family, it would be a sign of immaturity. It would be a sign of immaturity to refuse to accept help from other family members during a negative mood or depression. Keeping feelings inside causes us to lose our perspective. Unchecked depression, meanness, or moodiness spreads like wildfire in close living quarters and nesters need to be able to control these emotions or accept help in dealing with them.

Does nesting foster or hinder independence?

In the view of Jay Haley, author of *Leaving Home*, there's nothing wrong with the offspring who chooses to live at home. "Some people don't want to get married, and they stay with their parents until the parents get old, and then they care for them. If these offspring are working and doing something productive with their lives, it's perfectly reasonable. It's when someone stays at home and is chronically inadequate, always failing—and the parents always worrying about them and taking care of them—that it's pathological."[27]

There seems to be no clear-cut answer to the above question. Parents who answered our survey had differing views on this subject. Some parents who responded to the questionnaires were adamant in their belief that nesting fosters growth, and other parents were just as adamant that it hindered growth! Maybe the answer is as individual as each of us.

It's interesting to note the comments of those who believe that nesting fosters independence:

- One 22-year-old young lady wrote, "My parents have never put any obstacles in the way of my own decision-making."

- A mother of a 28-year-old son, who is a teacher, says, "He is a thoroughly responsible person. He's always done more than we ask of him and he does it on his own."

- A father writes that his son, who is 22-years-old, working and going to school, lives in a room off their recreation room. "It's far enough removed so that his coming and going is relatively unnoticed. As he attends school and works as well, he is seldom at home." (This son appears to live a life quite independent of his parents, even though they share the same house.)

Maturity is not bringing home the laundry.

• A mother of three adult offspring comments: "When they can make it on their own, they'll leave — all three of my children have finally left. I can't really believe that living at home is such a risk (of role stagnation). It seems to me...that a great many young peoples' problems are directly related to being on their own. They have complete freedom and tend to try drugs, alcohol, and sex because they have no one to make them feel uncomfortable about abusing these things."

• "Living at home gives offspring a good, secure background to use as a springboard in facing the world with confidence," says one mom.

• "Yes, our 31-year-old nesting daughter accepts the responsibilities of life. Yes, she helps around the house. She is part of our family! It also helps her career. You see, she is contemplating a job shift, away from the teaching profession. Because she is living at home, she is able to do some researching into different fields. We certainly recognize her as an adult — she's been an independent adult for over ten years. She has her own space and really only shares the conveniences of kitchen and laundry. She is decidedly a boarder and we have very little trouble with this since for seven years she was a very responsible, independent single person living and working away from home."

● "Both of our grown children who are living at home, George and Sherry, are independent enough. They take care of themselves."

● "I feel that having adult offspring living at home fosters their growth in four areas — responsibility, career, social life and a serious love relationship."

● "Commitment, self-control and self-discipline are often lacking in the growing process outside the family atmosphere. It's better for them to live at home."

● "Our son takes responsibility for his actions. He seems to get along socially. Living at home provides a home base for job seeking. Serious love relationship? Living at home helps to provide a family setting for accepting the girlfriend. If parents are responsible, children seem to follow suit."

The following true story is a prime example of one father who really enjoyed living, working and just being with his children — both when they were young and as they grew older. His grown children learned many skills while living at home which helped them become independent people. This father felt that, if there was no reason for them to stay, his children would leave home. So he planned one project after another to keep their interest. "Looking back," he wrote, "I can see that I spent most of my parenting years trying to avoid the day when any of the children would leave home."

His family lived in a small country home that had a barn. So he got horses (horses needed to be fed, ridden, cleaned, and housed). They had a fireplace (wood needed to be sawed, chopped, carried and fires needed to be tended). They lived on the coast of Maine, so they had boats (boats had to be hauled, caulked, and painted).

They reaped the benefits of the sea — both clams and eels. After that, the family turned to real estate. They bought and renovated old houses, barns and "woebegone buildings." They cleared trees, repaired, painted, sawed, and shingled houses. Their labor force grew during the summers until it numbered as high as sixty, including friends and neighbors who wanted to work to earn some money. "Finally, though, we ran out of needs and the children began to leave. Without needs there was no keeping the young." In short, he envied those farmers who were able to keep their sons and daughters — they had the home place to work for their entire lives![28]

The offspring in the above mentioned family were exposed to a wide variety of experiences which will ultimately help them lead independent lives. Surely, this man's children learned a great deal and grew in family closeness while they lived at home.

One of the benefits that some parents felt accompanied living at home was that their offspring didn't have to rush into, or cling to, a love relationship. They were getting plenty of normal family love.

One mother felt that growth toward independence and maturity was very individual. She said that they raised four sons, all now over 18 years. Noticeable growth and independence was different for each one. Two were very mature at age 18, but the other two were far from mature at that same age. Therefore, she felt that parents needed to observe each child individually to recognize their particular needs and respond to them, whether this meant living at home or outside the home.

Following are some comments by grown sons and daughters living at home who feel that this helps them in their growth:

- "I don't feel that living at home should adversely affect growth. One should have responsibilities even if one *is* living at home," says Barb, a 19-year-old nester.

- "Living at home while attending school in town did not in any way hinder my adjustment to living away from home when I decided to go out of town to continue my education. There just doesn't seem to be much difference. I plan to continue living at home after graduation until I either marry, relocate, or buy my own home," relates a 24-year-old male nester.

- "I am home because it is a way to save some money right now. And, you know, I still have my independence!" says a 26-year-old son.

- "It shouldn't affect the growth of independence," writes a 22-year-old son at home.

- "We function well as two independent units living together in the same house. I believe mine is a rather unique situation because I have lived independently away from home for seven years (she is now 31). I've always been prepared for responsibility and independence. None of my time at home has been at my parents' expense financially. I love to be with my family. I can see how family love grows when I'm living at home."

On the other hand, some people feel that nesting really does hinder growth. The following are comments from families with this view:

- "Some grown kids sponge off their folks and take advantage of them. We know one family where the man is retired and his wife works hard as a waitress. They have a son, 37-years-old, who is home collecting unemployment. He thinks that these parents are in effect saying, 'Go ahead, take advantage of us.' "[29]

- "I really think a child *has* to move out in order to grow up," one father relates.

- "It makes me mad when I think of my sister spending all her money on clothes and living off our folks!" says an older brother of a nester. "She gets all the breaks."

What about those nesters who seem to be stagnating?

Some parents feel that an adult offspring living at home risks role stagnation. They feel these nesters are surrounded by the environment of childhood and that makes it difficult for them to grow and move into a new adult role. One woman writes about a relative of hers, whom she feels fell into this role stagnation. This male relative, after his return home from World War II, lived with his parents until his father's death about twenty years ago. He continued to care for his mother for an additional five years, until she had to be placed in a nursing home, where she subsequently died. Following her death, he required counseling to cope with his guilt for placing her in a nursing home. Then, he had a series of girlfriends for about ten years, but refused to get married. This woman relative relating the story says, "Going home again for a brief time may be the answer sometimes, but in the long run it may not enable one to develop a true sense of independence. Mother made her nest as cozy as possible and then reaped her reward in her old age, but at what cost to her son?"

One magazine article stated that a few young adults "risk permanent grounding because of emotional dependency. 'I came home mostly for economic reasons,' sighs Ed, an unemployed political science graduate who has lived with his parents in Boston for the past five years, 'but I never got out.' "[30]

Psychiatrist Paul Kingsley wonders if we are doing our young adults a favor by letting them stay on more or less permanently at home. Are we stifling their growth? Perhaps he had in mind someone like the above sons who were deeply attached to their parents' home. This may be something that families should watch out for — an overdependence of the nester upon the family.

One nester, no longer young at 38, has lived with his parents as an adult since he was 24 years old. He feels it hinders his development in all areas of his life. Yet he writes that his parents recognize him as an adult, encourage him to solve his own problems, make his own decisions, and don't volunteer advice regarding his clothes, hair, and general appearance. But still, he feels that an adult offspring who lives at home definitely risks role stagnation! Apparently, he is stuck in the nesting role and can't force himself out of it.

Roberta Chaplan, a New York psychiatrist, claims a "child should learn to accept authority and as an adult eventually become his own authority. In some cases, that step is never taken and the children continue to rely on parents' rules and not on their own. In a crisis situation especially, or when a big decision must be made, they listen to other people instead of trusting their own judgement."[31]

One article states that for many adults a thread of dependency still ties them to their parents. "For some, this means being unable to make big decisions on their own. For others, it means being afraid to tell their parents how they feel about many things, and for still others it means continuing to look for ways to win the love and praise they enjoyed, or missed, as children.... Psychologists also say that many adults harbor fears from childhood that if they act in a way their parents disapprove of, the parents will abandon them or stop loving them."[32] A dangerous side effect to dependency is resentment.

One man, a 30-year-old writer, claimed his mother encouraged him to be dependent on her. "She never had a career and she needed to feel needed. One way (to fulfill her needs) was to take care of me. I guess I was so angry at myself for being in the position of feeling obliged to her that it came out in resentment towards her."[33] If parents are aware of this possible long-range effect, feelings of dependency can be avoided.

Some offspring are caught in role stagnation — inability to grow into independence — because of a crisis in their middle-aged parents' lives. The National Institute of Health conducted a study on thirty families with offspring entering adulthood. The offspring, because they were just getting started in life, had many options open in areas of work and love. Seeing this, many fathers seemed to regret the choices that they made in their own lives. Meanwhile, the mothers faced the prospect of an empty nest, with loss of their motherly role, as the offspring spoke of moving on. Thus, many of these mothers turned to their husbands for reinforcement of their own self-esteem. The husbands, however, were too wrapped up in thinking through their own life choices and results to notice the wives' needs.

After being rejected by their husbands, most of the wives reacted by turning back to their children. This motherly concentration upon the children's lives made it difficult for them to take the steps needed to launch out on their own. Often the result was a resigned father, an intrusive mother, and an abrupt and bitter exit by the offspring. Those offspring who remained at home had conflict, generally with their mother. In many of these thirty families, the offspring couldn't gain independence, form solid friendships, or obtain a job.[34]

Author Jay Haley feels that there is an identifiable reason why an occasional young person is constantly getting into trouble, either via drugs, crime, or paralyzing apathy — because of a need on the part of the offspring to preserve the family. He does this by sacrificing his own growth. The offspring's failure prevents parents from facing issues in their marriage that might lead to divorce. The offspring keeps the parents concentrating on his problems to the neglect of their own. The price that is paid is the lack of emotional growth in the offspring. The offspring, either consciously or subconsciously, refuses to succeed in his growth toward independence. Often this young person is not able to function in school, work, or close friendships. Some offspring fail just prior to the point of success — right before graduation, failing to find a job, losing one job after another, or taking menial jobs below his capabilities.[35]

The above type of offspring, as described by Haley, certainly is stuck in the rut of role stagnation. If parents were aware of this type of syndrome and recognized it in their own situation, possibly they would be motivated to take care of their marriage problems — freeing their offspring to develop at a normal rate. And, likely, the marriage would either improve or dissolve.

Conclusion

Becoming independent entails many actions on the part of the nester. It's an easy, gradual progress for some. It's a harder road for others. There are definite things that parents and nesters can do to foster growth toward independence. Nesting may foster or hinder growth toward independence depending on how parents and nesters act. If, however, families are aware of pitfalls, nesting can be a growing experience.

"Lately it's (been difficult) to communicate with my young people without degenerating into yelling. We're a generation apart and we think differently. When they're little, I can impose my will. But when they're bigger than I am, I have to use reason and that doesn't always work," says Vicky, a mother of a large family.
"But," replied her son, "that's because logic doesn't always apply to life's situations."[1]
—Vicky Debbins & son

CHAPTER V

Communications: So Let's Talk About It

Many young people living at home are in a state of transition or growth, which can cause pressure and tension for parents as well as children. In turn, this pressure and tension can make communication difficult. Therefore, the situation of nesting requires the wisdom of Solomon, the patience of Job and the kindness of a Saint — from the parents as well as the nester.

The secret of living with adult kids (or anybody) is communication. This chapter will cover various types of communication. It will also deal with specific topics relating to nesting that need open communication between nesting family members.

Communicating in Anger—Healed with Love

Hidden resentment can be a real problem behind blocked communication. Sometimes the only way to get hidden resentment out in the open is by direct conflict. Even though this is distasteful, it may be the only way to clear the air especially if there is long-standing resentment. The following example touchingly illustrates this point. Love then was able to restore the relationship. The Johnson's had two adult daughters living at home. Sue was 24 and Peggy was 19. In addition, there were two other children in the family. During their growing-up years, Sue and Peggy had shared a bedroom and bad feelings had begun then about neatness of the room, sharing clothes, and when to turn off the light — Sue was a reader and Peggy was not. These bad feelings were really never resolved, they had just simmered under the surface.

The parents knew that matters between the two were not getting better, and in fact were getting worse. One Sunday evening the parents returned home to find out that the daughters had had another disagreement that day. Later that evening the disagreement erupted into a violent shouting match. The rest of the family came running to see what could be done to stop it. But Sue and Peggy just continued to scream at each other.

Mother sat down and sank into despair. Father stood by and prayed silently. Then Bill, their 22-year-old son, began to weep softly. At first, no one noticed home. His spirit was overcome with great sadness at seeing his two sisters screaming hatred back and forth. Very quickly, Bill's weeping turned to great heaving sobs that Sue and Peggy could no longer ignore. They turned to Bill in an attempt to console him. But he was unable to stop and could not even talk, so great was his emotion. Then both sisters put their arms around Bill for he was a much-loved brother. Sue begged, "What can we do to make you stop crying, Bill?" He was unable to reply, so they could only hug him. In the process, he wrapped an arm around each sister and pulled them together. Soon Sue and Peggy were apologizing to each other. Then Rosie, the younger sister, ran to get hankies for the family, for everyone needed one by now.

All this took place two years ago. Sue and Peggy have had disagreements since, but the deep-rooted, long-standing resentment between the two seems to be gone. They can now talk about their differences as they arise.

Utilizing Body Language in Communication

The family who reads body language can use this information to relate to the emotional states of one another. If a family can't get problems out in the open, things just get worse.

Let's look at Kim. She was angry at her mother, because Kim thought her parents were spoiling the younger children. She felt that they were being treated better than she had been treated when she was younger. Janie, her little sister, has just gotten a new bicycle and Kim remembers how she had been given a second-hand one years ago when she was Janie's age. But Kim couldn't talk about it. So, one day she just didn't say good-bye before she left for work. Mother felt hurt at this obvious omission and in the back of her mind she knew that this was a red flag. Something was bothering Kim. The next morning Kim not only neglected to say goodbye, but she slammed the door as well. Matters weren't resolved that evening either and the following morning Kim slammed the door so hard the window next to the front door broke! Kim was not able to verbalize her anger, but she was saying loud and clear, "Hey, something you did bothers me!" By reading Kim's body language and responding to it, this mother could have used a shortcut in their communications and saved a window. She could have talked it out with Kim and found out what was bothering her. Then she could have said, "I'm sorry you feel we are playing favorites. But we have more money now than we did when you were little. We help you now in other ways. We did the best we could for you when you were little according to our income then."

We can utilize body language to help us get along with our

nesters by realizing that we act out our state of being with nonverbal language, says Julius Fast, author of *Body Language*. "We lift one eyebrow for disbelief. We rub our noses for puzzlement. We clasp our arms to isolate ourselves or to protect ourselves. We shrug our shoulders for indifference, wink one eye for intimacy, tap our fingers for impatience, slap our forehead for forgetfulness."[2]

The quickest and plainest kind of body language is touch. "The touch of a hand, or an arm around someone's shoulder, can spell a more vivid and direct message than dozens of words."[3]

Hugh Riordan, a psychiatrist in Wichita, Kansas, urges families to touch. "Try family back rubs," he urges. This helps loosen us up and gets the talk flowing. Lightly touch a child as you walk by or put your hand on an arm as you talk. This shows that you really care about the person you touch.

In order to encourage a nester to talk, the parent can sit, stoop, or slope his body. This shows empathy and will put a grown son or daughter on a more even footing with parent.[4] If, during a talk, you realize that the other person is sending some messages, leg swinging or foot or finger tapping, this is a cue that he/she is getting ready to leave. It's time to try to remove or lessen the tension if you want to continue to talk.

Drawn-in shoulders, Julius Fast says, means that the person is having suppressed anger, raised shoulders means fear, squared shoulders means that he is shouldering some responsibility, and bowed shoulders means that he is carrying a burden or a heavy load. A person with arms and legs crossed is saying that he feels a tightness and is withdrawn. Asking that person to uncross his legs and arms may help him open up and talk.[5]

By reading body language, we can get the talk flowing, bring out hidden resentments, and have a happier life with our nester. Communicating effectively, with whatever means at hand, including body language, is a worthy goal.

Pressures That Nesters Endure

Circumstantial pressures upon nesters may lead to a breakdown in inter-family communications. Where once the nester may have lived in harmony within the home when he was a child, now that he is an adult, problems may suddenly so intervene with responsibilities that open communications are in jeopardy. Difficulty in communicating with his parents, a failure grade at school, or a problem at work, could mean a difficult time for the whole family. Decisions about school, career, and/or marriage that will affect him throughout his entire life are generally made by an offspring while nesting. How these decisions are made can shape the relationship between nester and parents.

School. John, for example, has decided to go on to college, but he can't decide which one to attend. Application deadlines are near, the pressure is on for a decision. John is normally a loving, considerate family member, but because of these pressures, he has become uncommunicative and irritable. Lately, a typical scene with John is as follows. It's been hours since John came home from school and no one has seen or heard from him .Mother sends Sarah, a little sister, to find John and tell him that supper is ready. Sarah finds John in his room, and in response to her invitation, he snarls, "Tell Ma I'm busy and can't eat for another half hour!"

It is obvious that John needs some assistance in dealing with his college choice. A sympathetic parent can help alleviate some of his indecision by taking time to discuss with him what characteristics he should be considering when choosing a school. Some examples might be:

Size: Does he want a small, close-knit college atmosphere or a large and somewhat impersonal university setting?

Location: How far is it from home? Will the distance impair his ability to get home for vacations or long weekends? (Some freshman and sophomores come home once a month on scheduled three-day weekends. Some schools lock-up for these long weekends, forcing students to find a place to go.)

Public or Parochial: Does he want to be on a secular campus or have the relgious setting of a parochial school?

Curricula: Does the school have the courses and accreditation in the area he wants to study? If undecided, does the school have a wide variety of courses from which to choose? A variety of courses will help him narrow down his options for study.

Cost: How much can he afford, or how much can the parents afford to help him? (It is very important to discuss this, laying out clearly each party's responsibility.)

Type of school: College, university, two-year junior college, or trade/vocational school? Maybe a different type of school could satisfy the nester's requirements better than the school he thinks he would like to attend.

In addition to these basic considerations, it may be helpful here to go into depth on a few more which concern schooling decisions.

In view of inflation, we must expect and plan for rising education costs. One private college estimates that in ten years, costs will be four times the present charges. This may force the nester to remain living in his parents' home and commute back and forth to school in order to save money on room and board.

Also, since many parents did not attend college, they may not understand the trade school/college educational system. The following example should illustrate the need to know the facts about higher education. Donna had good grades all through high school and could easily have been admitted to any college. Several of her friends decided to attend the neighborhood community college, so Donna enrolled there too. Her parents didn't object because they were unaware that the business world does not view credits or degrees from community colleges as highly as university credits or degrees. Years later, because she had a degree from a community college, Donna was unable to obtain a coveted job. She lost out to another applicant, who had a university degree. Investigating all options before making a

Living at home means there is always someone who cares.

decision on schooling would prevent this type of thing from happening.

Some parents have their hearts set on a college degree for their children and are bitterly disappointed if they do not attend or complete college. But, some students who attempt advanced schooling find it too difficult and are forced to drop out. Rick, a college sophomore, smashed his fist through a large glass window on campus out of sheer frustration regarding his failing grades. This resulted in serious personal injury and expulsion from college. In addition, the suicide rate of college students is on the increase.[6] With this type of evidence, parents and nesters need to be honest with themselves and come to a decision on whether a degree is really desirable in their case. The Bureau of Labor estimates that one out of four college graduates will have to settle for a job beneath his expectations because there are more diplomas than the economy can support. Some college graduates feel that the time and money they expended on getting a degree was unnecessary.

From the statistics below, we can see that a significant percentage of people are entering the work force immediately after high school graduation. (This does not mean, however, that they will not return to formal schooling later. After a year or two, they may decide to re-enroll.)

- 31.2% of our high school graduates each year go on to college.[7]
- 17% enroll in a vocational or technical school each year.[8]
- 43% will attempt to enter the job market on a full-time basis.[9]

In conclusion, nesters have a choice to make about a school or job. But, help in this decision may be necessary, so talk about it! If you do, everyone will feel better and know what to expect from each other. Even though there may be disappointment on the part of parents if their child drops out of school or wants to attend a trade school instead of a four-year college, parents should realize that millions of other parents and nesters are suffering through the same choices and decisions. There is often an upward mobility from generation to generation. The son gets more schooling and a better job than his father. But upward mobility is not *always* the case, and not always necessary.

Job Hunting. This may be another pressure with which your nester has to grapple. If he has decided to enter the work field rather than continue a formal education, he may need help in deciding what he wants to do and where he should look for work. Jobs are usually found through word of mouth, want ads, and private or governmental agencies. Emotional support is definitely needed while one is job hunting, especially during times of high unemployment. This can be a tedious, ego-deflating, and emotionally depressing experience. Job hunting is a time when a nester needs an extra boost.

One father relates a clear and concise approach for helping a nester in the job hunt. He says, "We sometimes think that a young person can just go out and get a job. However, he needs help and encouragement at a very early age to help him in applying for jobs. It's never easy to make that first big step, and most children will resist every effort when you try to encourage them to get a job. They make remarks like, 'I am grown up and I can do this in my own time,' or 'I want to have my youth; I'm not ready to get a job yet,' or 'All you ever think about is getting me to go to work.' "

The father continues. "The kids leave us, their parents, with terrible guilt feelings saying that we are pushing them out to work too soon. Yet, we know that what they are really saying is, 'I'm scared. What will the employer say to me? How much should I ask for in pay? What happens if he says no?'

"We, as parents, should be allowing our children, while they are young, to learn that they will need to earn a living somehow. Perhaps as soon as age 14 they should be applying for a part-time job. This will help them get used to prospective employers saying 'no,' and also hopefully know the satisfaction of an employer saying, 'Yes, I'll hire you. When can you start?' Getting a variety of job experiences is extremely helpful in deciding what type of job or profession they might desire in the future. As a parent, we have the responsibility of helping them through this stage of their lives. They need our input as to what their abilities and talents are — as we see them. This knowledge will help them when they need to consider a profession to fit their talents, skills, and abilities or when they need to make decisions regarding advanced schooling."

In general, the state of transition or growth that many

nesters are in tends to make them fearful, anxious and ill-tempered. They are apt to take their frustrations out on the people closest to them, the ones they love the most. At this time, communications are extremely important, but are often difficult to maintain. If the pressures of school or job become too great, some young adults take subconscious refuge in anxiety, illness, depression and a few even become suicidal. Concern from a loving family will often turn the tide for them.

Social Life. Some nesters come under severe pressure regarding their social life. It seems that either they are overly busy or there is nothing to do. There are problems in either case. If their social life is too busy, their time is taken up with dates, dances, and parties. Then family responsibilities (both household chores and family communications) suffer. If their social life is nil, then the nester can go into a depression and use the family home as an escape — rather than seeking out old friends or making new ones. How is a nester to find the right balance? A word from parents can alert a nester to the fact that he's getting too busy or that he's stagnating. Then appropriate action should be taken. If it's a busy time, the nester should cut back and get reacquainted with the family. If it's a lonely time, nester should make an effort to get involved in some outside activity.

An example of being too busy is 20-year-old Shelley, who has just made up with her steady boyfriend, Tom, after a disturbing quarrel. Night after night now Shelley waves good night to the family as she and Tom spend every free minute together. Shelley's responsibilities at home are neglected, leading to problems with her parents. Three days in a row she has brushed aside Mom's ever-increasing requests to, "Please do *something* with your room today, Shelley. You know Grandma is coming to visit this

---

Author's note: An excellent resource for career exploration and choice is *What Color Is Your Parachute?* by Richard Nelson Bolles.

weekend." But Shelley only gives an agreeable answer, "Yes, later" as she runs out the door.

Then there's Mike. He is stagnating. Several of his friends recently left for college, and another buddy is going steady with a special girl. So Mike finds himself suddenly without friends. He stays home night after night, watching television and snacking. He's gaining weight at an alarming rate. Realizing that Mike needs a new interest, Dad suggests he join a bowling team or take dance lessons.

Many nesters are experiencing pressures regarding school, job, and social life. An awareness of these pressures is a first step in relieving them. Support from parents can go a long way in helping to relieve these pressures. If stress can't be relieved, then just sharing them with a caring family will often help the situation.

Pressures That Parents Endure

Having an adult offspring in the house can cause all sorts of pressures on parents. What's a parent to do about household chores, use of the car, going to church, etc. if there is disagreement as to who is to do what and when. In this section, we will look at various topics that have caused pressures on parents which, in turn, inhibit communication.

In our survey, topics mentioned that created differences between parents and nesters were:

Transportation
Religious activities
Recreation
Household chores
Job hunting
Sex
Rearing of a grandchild
Carelessness with clothes
Nester's friends
Nester's lack of job or schooling
Late sleeping
Kitchen use after hours and failure to clean up
Lack of personal cleanliness

Uncommunicativeness
Disagreements about politics, investments, and trends
Jealousy
Despondency
Rock music
"Pot"
Nester's choice of vocabulary
Constant feelings of having to be careful not to irritate each other
Friends of nesters invading the home too often
Nester's treatment of siblings
Dirty dishes left around house
Unpaid long distance phone bills
Nester's general appearance
Refusal to take care of mail
Borrowing money
Smoking in the home

Since many of these are interrelated, they are dealt with generally in the following section, called "Bill of Rights." Some irritants are treated individually since they seem to be common concerns for many families.

Unsolicited Advice from Nesters on How to Raise Younger Siblings. The following family incident shows how two nesters felt they had spotted a problem and told their mother how to solve it. "One Sunday," writes a mother of eight children, "Two of the older girls, Mary and Kathy, had come to me separately to say how upset they were about Sam, their 15-year-old brother. He had gotten a job and had bought a moped. Mary felt that Sam had gotten "pretty egotistical now that he had his own money." Kathy said that because Sam was now the oldest son at home (two older brothers had recently moved out), he thought this gave him the rights and freedoms that his older brothers had had when they lived at home. She complained that he wasn't helping around the house anymore and that he was staying out late at night — much too late for a 15-year-old! She suggested he should do his fair share of work at home and come in earlier at night. In other words, the older sisters felt that mother should lay out some rules for Sam.

"When Mary complained about Sam, I just shrugged it off," wrote the mother. "But later, when Kathy did the same,

I told everyone, 'It looks like we have to have a family conference. It'll be tonight!' Later, around the dining room table, Mary and Kathy aired their complaints about Sam for fifteen long minutes. 'Okay, you two,' replied Sam, 'is it my turn now?' Then he gave his side of the story. His job took many of his formerly free hours, so some of Kathy's charges were true — he wasn't helping around the house as much as before. But Mary and Kathy had to realize that they only worked forty hours a week, while he attended school full-time and in addition was working fifteen hours a week as a busboy. Some nights he had to work till closing at 1:00 a.m., so that's why he was out late. It followed then that he slept late on weekends and missed out on some of the Saturday household chores. 'Sure I've got more money now,' continued Sam, 'but I worked hard for it, so I think that I can spend it on some things that I need and want — like my moped that I use to get to work.'

"There was some arguing back and forth," the mother continued writing. "At one point Kathy wanted to go to her room, but Dad wouldn't let her. I was getting discouraged over the bickering. But Dad just sat back and listened. Finally, an hour later, the air had cleared and they were all talked out. Resentments dissolved because nothing was left to brew inside the girls." With open communication, it was possible to resolve the festering resentments the older sisters were feeling and had expressed. Family discussions are not always easy nor pleasant, but are definitely necessary in restoring good feelings between young and older siblings.

Checking In. Neglecting to inform the people with whom you live about your timetable can cause concern and worry. It is only common consideration for nesters to inform their family if they are not planning on eating or sleeping at home some night. Checking in makes for a smooth-running home.

Dr. Joyce Brothers has some good advice regarding how to solve the problem of checking in for meals. One mother was having a problem with her 22-year-old daughter because she didn't let her mother know her dinner plans. Dr.

Brothers assumed that mother and daughter had talked this over without success. She then went on to suggest possible causes that the mother could take into consideration, e.g. working late, or last minute invitations from a boyfriend. However, it may just be that the daughter had fallen into a bad habit. Dr. Brothers suggests that the daughter check in with her mother each day, as late as conveniently possible, to inform the latter of her dinner schedule.[10]

As far as checking in regarding sleeping goes, this is more serious than checking in regarding meals. When a nester doesn't come home as expected, this can cause real worry for the parents. Here's what happened when a nester didn't inform her parents in advance of her overnight plans.

Ellen had been to a party with her boyfriend and during the course of the evening, she and a girlfriend made plans for early the next morning. To them it made sense for Ellen to sleep over at her girlfriend's house. So, at midnight, Ellen's boyfriend went home and Ellen and her girlfriend went on to Ellen's home to get some clothes for the next day. Then, so her parents wouldn't worry, she made a large note — two feet by three feet — telling her parents of her plans. She taped this note to her bedroom door. Ellen's mother woke up at around 3:00 a.m. and realized that she hadn't heard Ellen come in to say that she was home. She got up to check Ellen's bedroom. In the darkness she walked right past the oversized note and on into the empty bedroom. Panicking, she woke her husband and they called Ellen's boyfriend's parents, who said that their son had come home hours ago. They didn't know where Ellen was. Ellen's parents worried and prayed for several hours. Finally at 6:00 a.m., they called the police. Walking down the hallway to answer the policeman's knock, they passed their daughter's bedroom and in the early dawn light they saw her note. All those agonizing hours need not have happened if Ellen had woken her mother when she stopped at home at midnight or, better yet, had made her plans in advance and informed her parents of the plans ahead of time.

Transportation. Cars, bikes, and buses (transportation in general) are often an area of disagreement between nesters and their parents. Should the nester get his own car? If so, what kind of model and year made? If nester has his own car, there is generally no problem, unless nester runs short of gas money or can't make his monthly car payment. However, it's a different story if nester needs to use a family vehicle.

How does the family go about sharing time, gas expense, and shopping chores? It may be helpful to see how other families handle this problem.

Plans can be made in advance, so that optimal use is made of the car. If a nester needs to use the family car to go to work, and if mother needs to have a package delivered to her aunt's home near nester's place of work, it seems only reasonable that the nester deliver the package. But it is not reasonable if mom waits till the last moment and tells nester while he's going out the front door. Dropping off the package may make him late for work. The key to sharing a car is advance planning, stating needs ahead of time so that no one needs to be greatly inconvenienced.

When a nester uses a family car, several arrangements can be made to share gas expenses. Some parents charge their nester a flat fee per mile driven when he uses the family car. Other parents only ask that their nester replenish the gas he uses. A few parents hand their offspring the family gasoline charge card, intending them to use it wisely and pay their share of the bill.

Household Chores. "A thousand and one excuses the kids have got — math or baseball — not to do their jobs," says Vicky, a mother of 15 children. Getting cooperation from family members for household chores is often a difficult task, especially from nesters. It seems like there are never enough hands to do the jobs that need to be done. With some planning, this problem can be lessened. Being very specific in who does what, and when they do it, seems to

work best for most families. Work sheets listing various jobs
can be posted in a prominent place. The refrigerator door is
a good place to post this list since everyone seems to check in
there fairly often. One family's list reads thus:

> Joan: wash breakfast dishes
> Liz: sweep back stairs and basement
> Nathan: collect and bring dirty clothes to the basement
> Martina: sort and fold clothes
> Stefan: wash supper dishes and clean dining room
> John: make beds, vacuum living room and stairs.[11]

One mother is retaining responsibility for her household
by saying, "It's my duty as the parent to supervise my
children. They live in this house and are responsible for
some upkeep. It requires an effort, but I think each family
can devise its own method."[12]

However, there are some nesters who rarely help around
the home unless asked specifically to do so. One nester even
replied, "I shouldn't have to help around the house because,
after all, I pay rent." Fortunately, most nesters do help with
household chores. They have been known to help in the
following ways:

cleaning	house repair
laundry	garbage removal
cooking	care of pets
painting	garage upkeep
house & plant sitting	car care
lawn care	shopping

In delegating responsibility for chores around the home,
it's important to be fair. A busy nester is not going to have as
much free time to work around the home as a sibling who
has the summer off and has time on his hands. This is why
it's so important to set up a schedule of duties together that
will fit in with you and your nester's lifestyle.

If you do set up such a schedule, perhaps then your nester
will cooperate with household chores as the following nester
does. He writes, "I do anything I can to help my Mom —
she's overworked!"

Religious Activities. The church gives the family a code of morals and invests it with a touch of holiness that helps keep it stable. 'The family that prays together stays together.'[13]

Convictions about God and church vary from family to family. It cannot be denied, though, that belief in God and religion play an integral part in many families. One mother tells how she views God. "I have a personal intimacy with God. I don't believe He's a blob in the sky bye 'n bye. It's like a marriage. One day you love Him, and the next day you have a fight with Him. What happens in the kitchen shakes the heavens. I tell my kids, I believe that what happens in this life affects eternity! Perhaps Maria, my daughter, says it even more clearly, 'We've got a God in our house and we use Him.' "[14]

When nesters and their families agree on religious beliefs and practices, then the nesting time can be very satisfying spiritually. This was true for about half of the families contacted in our survey.

But, of course, not all families agree on religious activities. When this occurs, it is important to communicate preferences and then discuss how to deal with them. Religious conviction and belief in a living, active God is a step which no one can force upon another person. Each person must be free to choose. If a grown offspring is forced to accompany the family to church, there isn't much spiritual value for either the nester or his family. God gave man a free will, and grown children, as well as everyone else, must be free to make their own decision in this regard. If parents are concerned about the example being given to younger siblings by a nester not attending church, then a good family discussion may be in order. If, as a parent of a nester, you feel that God is important, then perhaps by your actions and loving acceptance — not condemnation — you will have an influence on those with whom you live.

House Rules. House rules are a big problem for some nesting families. Who *does* have the final say, parents or

nester? From the consensus of research, it does seem that the
parents should have the final say. As one daughter says, "I
don't try and change my mom's ideas anymore. After all,
this is her territory."

One dad says, "Young people grow up in a home and they
come to feel it is theirs. In a sense it is theirs, but unless you
as a parent take authority over the actions of the residents,
there will be no order. If there is no order, chaos can result.
Be gentle, but firm." He continues, "There should be
guidelines for young adults to follow, such as:

- You can eat after meals, if you clean up the kitchen.
- You can have friends over and, within reason, they can use the
  food in the house.
- You can have your own bedroom or share one with a brother or
  sister, but you have to take responsibility to keep it clean and
  neat.
- You have your rights as one of our children, but your rights
  not to infringe upon the rights of other family members."

Professional advisors also agree that it's best if there are
firm guidelines. "Neubauer (a marriage therapist in New
York) is firm about insisting that if such an arrangement
(nesting) becomes necessary, the group should work out
every detail in advance — chores, finances, and even at what
point an amicable separation needs to take place.
'Otherwise, just deciding who is supposed to take out the
garbage could become a major disaster,' she said. 'Everyone
must know exactly what is expected of the others.' "[15]

One mother came right to the point. "This is a family.
This is not a hotel where you come and go. Even if you're an
adult...you have to abide by the rules.... If you guys think
you're going to eat and sleep here and spend all your money
on stereos and cars, you have another cookie coming.
Because then I feel I'm being used by my kids. I'm a very
compassionate woman, but I'm not a sucker."[16]

Parents' Bill of Rights
(written by a father of several nesters)

1. Expect help from nesters with household and yard chores in the amount of ½ hour per day plus 2 hours on Saturday or their day off.

2. Expect contribution according to nesters' means toward their room and board.

3. Expect nesters to keep their area (bedroom) of the house clean daily.

4. Expect nesters to abide by the rules of the home regarding smoking and drinking and inform their visiting friends of these rules also.

5. Expect nesters to be communicative and respectful to other family members.

6. Expect nesters to be participating members of the family—meals, recreation, etc.

Nesters' Bill of Rights
(written by a 22-year-old nester)

1. Deserves respect from parents as an adult.

2. Deserves respect from parents regarding the decisions he makes—that they are decisions made by an adult, rather than decisions made by a minor.

3. Parents must be willing to give a nester the needed independence to grow as an adult, i.e., don't smother a nester and prevent him from developing into his full potential.

Siblings' Bill of Rights
(written by three siblings of a nester)

1. The grown-up kids living at home should respect the privacy of the younger kids.

2. The grown-up kids should get the same treatment as the other kids—no special favors for them because they are grown-up.

3. The big kids shouldn't tell their brothers and sisters what to do, or tell their parents how to raise the other kids.

"The rural family in Ireland lives, on the average, on a farm too small to be subdivided any further, and therefore only one son can inherit the land. The father can pick any one of them he likes, but he does not indicate his choice until he is good and ready. The result is that the sons who do not emigrate or drift off to jobs in the cities stay home and go on working, in a position of total subordination to the old man. And if they should get a side job like road mending, their wages are supposed to go into their father's pocket, and he is quite capable of turning up himself on payday to collect whatever money they may have earned."[1]

CHAPTER VI

Money Matters —
It Really Does

The financial reasons for our kids staying at home or returning to it, and the parents' responsibility for training their nesters in money matters, are two big problems when adult kids are living at home. The most highly volatile money issues are room and board, checking accounts, budgets, loans, health insurance, and taxes. We really need a lot of love and communication to get through this money maze!

Recession and Inflation

Yesterday, today — and probably tomorrow — the majority of nesters come home, or stay home, on a temporary or a permanent basis, because of money matters. Today, the twin financial problems of inflation and recession are especially burdensome for our young people.

This may be their first exposure to the fact that the value of a dollar has been decreasing steadily for the past few years. They're learning one economic truth the hard way: with inflation, we need more money, but it buys less. A growing number of young people are discovering that independence is beyond their means. "My salary just doesn't keep up with inflation. I don't want to live in some cheap apartment house," writes one young woman. "So I live with my folks, even though it's not what I prefer." Many young adults have grown up with a high standard of living. They are used to affluence, reports Psychiatrist Paul Kingsley. To leave their parents' home and support themselves fully, means they'd have to live on a lower standard. They're not as willing to do that as earlier generations were.[2] But many nesters just can't afford both high apartment rent and monthly car payments. Another economics lesson they're quickly learning is that in a recession, businesses are forced to lay off employees because of cutbacks in production.

A few nesters are unemployed and forced to rely on their parents for room and board. Because they're young, they are the victims of "last hired, first fired." Some student and low-salaried working nesters also need support from their parents. This comes as a shock to some parents who never thought that their grown child might need help with everyday living expenses. But, times have changed since today's parents of nesters were in their twenties.

Legally, our financial obligation to our children ends when they reach eighteen. We've fed and clothed them, we've paid for eye glasses, orthodontists, schooling, and in some cases, car and college expenses. On top of all this, we've loved them with all our hearts. "Isn't that enough?" some parents ask. "Just how far do we have to carry this kid? We've just started thinking of retirement and travel plans and along comes our grown kid who needs money. Are we supposed to sacrifice our retirement dreams, our dreams of freedom, so we can bail him out?"

But, who can say "no" to a son or daughter who needs a

place to hang his hat — either for financial or emotional reasons? How can we refuse him a car loan or help with his college expenses if he needs it and we have the means? How can we say "no" without feeling guilty? And if we do say "yes," can we really say it without a trace of resentment?

Studies show that money is high on the list of factors for causing trouble in a family. We hear and talk about the breakdown of communications, the drug and alcohol problems, and the behavior problems with our children. However, unspoken money problems are the most volatile issues to trigger hot tempers within a family. And they are set up by ignorance and insensitivity. One nester indicated on the survey that he had "no idea" of the amount of his parents' combined annual income. How can he be expected to be sympathetic to their financial problems if he isn't aware of their financial obligations along with their income?

Sometimes, the only way to resolve conflict is to bring it out in the open.

A Spirit of Ungratefulness

Three fathers personally conveyed to the author their feelings of resentment against their nesters. Not only aren't the kids contributing for room and board, but one dad is footing all college expenses. The fathers felt their offspring were ungrateful. One father, Ed, stated that, "Not asking for room and board was the biggest single mistake I have made with my five grown children who freely move in and out." He feels that not asking for room and board gave his kids the idea that he has lots of money. So now, not only do they not pay room and board, but they also ask him for extra money when they run short of cash. If he had been more open with his children about how much money he made, and about his fixed monthly expenses, he feels the problem would have been avoided.

Mel, the second father, is a classic example of a parent who sacrificed his own personal wants in order to save money for his kids' expenses. For one son, he footed the bills through an undergraduate degree, a master's degree, and a doctorate. He also frequently sent $100 money orders for extra expenses, when his son asked for it. Yet, after all this financial help, the son didn't acknowledge his indebtedness. One day his son came home and, during a conversation with his dad, claimed that he never received any financial help from his father! Perhaps the argument was based on a misunderstanding. However, this denial of his help, and the underlying ingratitude, has made Mel bitter towards his son. He now suggests that a parent save all receipts and cancelled checks so he can later prove his financial assistance, if necessary.

Jerry is another resentful father who feels that his children take him, and his money, for granted. "It's as if they feel they have a God-given right to my support," he says. But Jerry believes that there is nothing in his paternal contract that says he has to give money to grown children, especially when they don't even say "thank you."

The best way to ease these growing tensions is through communication between parents and offspring. By talking about their feelings and opinions, they may smooth tension and resentment on both parts. It may turn out that our kids are simply so unsophisticated and ignorant about money matters, that we aren't looking at the issue of money through the same eyes.

Perhaps we should start with the financial education of our children. If you haven't communicated honestly in the past about this subject, now is a beautiful time to begin! Start by talking about money in general. It'll be the first step towards making life with your nesters free from under-the-surface financial tensions. Build up to talking about those hidden resentments and unresolved money problems. Bring it all out into the light. Let them know where the money comes from and where it goes, month by month. Discuss the financial goals and objectives of both parents and nesters. Talk about budgeting, loan agreements, grocery and utility bills, school expenses, checking accounts, health insurance, taxes, and most of all, the specific financial sacrifices of the parents for their children without seeming to throw it in their faces. If we guide the financial education of our own children as they grow, we can avoid a lot of ungratefulness and resentment about money while our children are in the nester stage. If, after our children have reached adulthood, and they still seem to be unaware of our true financial situation, correct the misimpressions and they won't expect too much financial aid.

Room and Board

The number one controversial financial issue between a nester and his parents is the subject of room and board. Some parents feel guilty for wanting their nester to help with room and board. After all, we don't want to squeeze blood out of a turnip, especially if it's our own turnip! Yet, we don't want to be used financially, or to be unappreciated for

all the things we've given our children. Imagine being the
parent who heard "through the grapevine" that her nester
son was bragging to his friends about the "free ride" he was
getting by living at home. As tempers flew, so did the nester
with all his belongings — right out the back door!

In our survey, only about two-thirds of the nesters who
are working full-time pay room and board. The average
amount paid is $75 a month, with a range of $40 to $200 a
month. This means that about a third of the nesters who are
working full-time pay no room and board at all. Hardly any
of the nesters who are students, either full- or part-time, pay
room and board.

To pay or not to pay—that is the question. All this
leads up to the question: should a nester pay room and
board? If he has a job, and if his parents don't feel they can
absorb the extra costs his presence creates, it becomes an
easy question to answer: obviously, yes. But if the nester has
even a low-paying job, and if the parents are fairly well
established, the answer is no longer so clear cut.

There were various reasons why some of the nesters do
not pay room and board:

"Dad won't take it," wrote one young man.
"He usually doesn't have enough money," replied a mother.
"Never discussed," responded another mother.

One parent replied, "She's not paying anything. She was
never asked to contribute." In the following instance both
son and mother gave their opinions on the subject. It was
interesting to see and compare their ideas on room and
board. This nester is 26 years old, attending school part-time
and working part-time, with an annual income of $8,000.
He felt that his parents didn't want room and board from
him. However, his mother had a slightly different view. She
wrote, "He feels we don't need the money and he does."
(This family was in an upper income bracket.) Often this
lack of room and board from a nester is a source of
irritation, and is frequently due to a lack of communication.

The following example indicates the beneficial results of talking about this problem. Sandi, who is working full-time and is concerned about helping out financially in the family home, has never been asked for room and board. Yet she doesn't want to be financially dependent on her family. She also wants to continue living at home. Her parents never talked about money to Sandi, and she knew that they would be very reluctant to accept any room and board payment. So, she decided she would talk to her mother, and carefully bring up the subject. She started off by asking about the household expenses. Because Sandi was showing an interest in the family finances, the conversation gradually got around to the subject of room and board. Sandi explained that she didn't want to be financially dependent on her folks, that she wanted to be treated as a responsible adult. Her mother came to understand and accept this fact, and soon her father did also. Today Sandi is paying room and board, equal to what it would cost her to live in a nearby apartment (including rent, utilities, food and laundry expenses). Her parents view Sandi with more respect now, and Sandi is satisfied that, even though she chooses to live in her parents' home, she is certainly paying her own way.

Here's another example of a satisfactory solution to the room and board problem. When the Brown's decided to ask their daughter, Paula, for room and board, she was agreeable to the suggestion. Paula had been feeling a trifle guilty that she had not been paying her folks anyway, so when they brought up the subject, Paula felt relieved because she hadn't known how to bring up the matter. She knew that her take-home pay was very little, but she would be getting two substantial raises within the next year. So, rather than setting a flat room and board fee now, and having to readjust it later when Paula's income increased, they all agreed to 15 percent of Paula's take-home pay as her room and board payment. In this family, talking about the situation eased the tensions and solved the problem for everyone.

Unfortunately, not all offspring are as willing as Paula and Sandi to contribute their fair share. If you are getting the feeling that your son or daughter might not be as willing to contribute as the two nesters above, read on. The following family story portrays a nester reluctant to contribute towards his keep. His response even bordered on belligerence. The Gaberg's 22-year-old son, Ben, was a rerooster who had returned home after college graduation. He has been back in the family nest now for over a year, and has been steadily employed all that time. Even though his job was at an entry-level position with the customary low pay, Mr. and Mrs. Gaberg talked over the matter privately and decided that Ben should start contributing towards room and board. One day Mrs. Gaberg broke the news to Ben. She was met by a frozen stare. Ben asked belligerently, "How much do ya want?" "Well," Mom replied, "I think it's something that we should talk about. Dad and I just aren't sure how much." However, Ben was unwilling to talk about it. "When you decide, let me know," he snarled and stomped out of the house. Several days later, after serving Ben's favorite supper, Mrs. Gaberg tried to talk to Ben again. She told him that she and Dad were serious about room and board, and had Ben given it any further thought? His reply was, "Ya, I suppose I havta if you guys say so. How much do ya want?"

Now Ben was reluctantly agreeable, but an amount had to be determined. "Let's look at how much take-home pay you get each month, Ben," Mom replied. "We don't want it to be a hardship on you, but we do feel that you should be paying something." Mrs. Gaberg picked up pencil and paper and wrote down Ben's monthly take-home pay, which was $600. Then she asked him to write down his fixed monthly expenses, which totaled $253, leaving him $347 on which to live. Ben was surprised that the remainder was so much. He had no idea where it all went! Mom suggested Ben pay $15 a week for room and board (she had discussed this privately with her husband and this is what they had agreed upon, if it was acceptable to their son). Ben's payment to his parents would total $60 a month, and in the light of the extra $347 Ben now realized he had, $60 didn't look out of line. It would still leave him with $287 each month to do with as he pleased. At the same time, he would have a feeling of paying his own way.

The Gaberg's communicated effectively by confronting their nester with the issue. If lack of room and board is a problem in your family life, but you have not been able to deal with it, consider the reasons why you may want to ask for room and board. Do you need the money to help meet the bills? If the answer is yes, the request is not based on greed, it is a necessity. But if you don't need the extra money, consider this. Are you preparing your nester to live outside your home in the real world of high prices?

Perhaps you are not doing your nester a favor by sparing him or her the financial responsibility of paying room and board, if he has an income, or could be earning an income. By not paying, we allow our nester to slide into a higher standard of living than they may be able to maintain later when they are on their own. Consequently, you may be forcing your nester to stay on in your home longer than may be good for all concerned. For all these reasons, nesters with low-paying or part-time jobs may especially need the responsibility of paying room and board — ironic as it seems — if for no other reason than to prepare them for the high costs of paying for their own basic needs later when they do move out.

It seems to be that the less income the parents make, the more often (and in larger amounts) the nester pays room and board. For example, one survey family's annual income was $14,000 and their nester paid $100 monthly. Another family, whose annual income was in the $100,000 range, did not require a room and board payment. The parents didn't need the additional income, so it was difficult for them to justify asking for room and board. Thus, it seems easier for low and middle income parents to educate their children in financial independence.

The following four cases illustrate how some families handle the room and board issue.

- The Smith's had two nesting daughters, in addition to eight other children. These two daughters pay the electric bill between themselves, which usually amounts to about $20 a week for each of them.

- One male nester, age 26 years old, is currently laid off. But when he is working he pays room and board every other week, on his pay day, in the amount of $100 per paycheck.

- Two brothers, age 22 and 25, both working full-time, "pay $10 to $15 a week depending on wages and whether lunches are packed and dinner served regularly."

- The fourth nester is 38 years old, male, with no siblings. He pays all home bills except mortgage payments, house insurance and phone. This means that he pays the electric bills, home repair bills, and taxes. In addition, he pays room and board of $50 to $75 a month. He is an older nester, more established in his job and can contribute more than younger nesters.

However, some parents don't feel they can ask for room and board when their nester is going to college, even if he is working too. It's usually true that nesters who are students have little or no extra money for room and board; that's why many of them are living at home. To insure a feeling of worth, appreciation and respect, however, how about another contribution — in the form of doing household chores? Here are some examples: Dale is a 19-year-old, full-time student with a part-time job. He has agreed to scrub and wax the kitchen floor and wash down the outside of the cupboards each week in exchange for room and board, in addition to straightening his room and helping with the dinner dishes every evening. Tammy and Joan, 19 and 20 years old, are both working part-time and attending school part-time. They "don't pay room and board directly," writes their mother, "but they do extra work for us around the house, such as laundry, heavy duty cleaning, and shopping."

Still other nesters are paying off school debts. For example, Jim, a college graduate, worked part-time while going to school but still had been forced to take out a loan to pay his tuition. After graduation, Jim didn't like the loan hanging over his head and wanted to get it paid off as quickly as possible. He discussed this with his parents and they said that he could live at home, rent-free, as long as he paid $300 a month on his college loan. Since his degree enabled him to secure a good job, he was able to make this large monthly payment. With his parents' help of a rent-free room, he was able to reduce his loan balance by a substantial amount each month.

Many nesters are living in their parents' homes because of upward mobility. Phil Donahue described it thus: "Remember the traditional Norman Rockwell view of America? The parents got out of the boat at Ellis Island and made their way up the street. The father worked hard and he and his wife sent their children out to the world to do better than they did. Well, most of the people in our generation did better than our parents. Not because we were smarter, but because we had a society that seemed to absorb us and give us more opportunities than our folks had, and in many cases there was less prejudice. Our parents wanted us to do better than they did and we want our kids to do better than we did."[3] But this attitude often means that a young adult will have to rely on his parents for a prolonged amount of time.

Some nesters are saving money for big-ticket items, such as a down payment on a home. Take the example of Sally and her family: Sally's marriage to Tom had broken up, leaving her feeling rejected, despondent, and nearly penniless. In addition, her 2-year-old daughter, Joni, was an added financial responsibility, though she was also a ray of sunshine for Sally. The young mother wanted to save money for a down payment on a little two-bedroom house that she visualized for herself and Joni. Her parents were glad to help them out with temporary, free housing while Sally was in this state of transition. They not only helped their daughter financially, but emotionally as well, with this embracing gesture. They felt that had they insisted on rent, this would only have delayed the day when Sally could realize her dream of a home for herself and her child.

A Special Category—Summertime College Nesters. Some nesters are periodic live-ins. College kids fall into this category. They come home for Christmas break, interim break, and summer. Most of them work during the summer and save their check to pay for the next year's tuition. Few families expect this category of nester to pay room and board. But other arrangements can be worked out, such as a sharing of household chores. This is really necessary when a family has several college-age kids who often arrive with a bang—hungry, loaded with dirty laundry, extra clothes, and furniture. To complete the picture, they also bring with them an increase in the noise level in the house: loud voices, blaring stereos, and a phone ringing off the hook! (How do their friends seem to know the very hour of their arrival?) It's an exciting time of getting together again, sharing events of months past and seeing a new maturity in the kids. But it's still a shock having them home again. With kids away at college, parents get used to a certain quietness, a gentle, prevailing peace. Then, suddenly, it's bedlam! A happy bedlam, but confusion nevertheless. Dad can't find his shorts, socks, newspaper, milk, or car. Yet he is forever tripping over clothes, friends, and shoes!

Along with all this confusion comes extra work, such as additional grocery shopping, cooking, laundry, and cleaning. It only seems right that these periodic nesters assume some share of the extra household chores. The Olson family currently has three college-age kids who come home each spring. After the initial greetings and exchanges of news and feelings, they divide up the summer chores. Last summer, Mary offered to keep the two cars in clean condition and do the grocery shopping. Pete volunteered for the yard work. Ginger kept the washing machine loaded and the clean clothes neatly folded into proper piles. With this happy arrangement and relatively easy workload, there was time to enjoy each other's company for the next few months, without squabbles. Mom and Dad knew too that it would be as quiet as a morgue again come September. In one way, they'd miss all the frenzied summer activities. But just as soon as they'd begin to really enjoy the quiet, it would be time for Christmas to roll around and the kids would be back....

Families who don't talk about room and board may suffer the fate of the Bonel family. Here were traditional parents willing to help out, but who, through lack of communication about finances, were pushed to the limit and reacted in the extreme. A real estate agent related the following tale.

Mr. and Mrs. Bonel contacted this realtor, saying that they wanted to put their home up for sale and buy a smaller one with only one bedroom. They presently had a medium-priced home with four bedrooms. Their children were all grown, but they had a tendency to keep moving back in, without paying their way. The first time the married daughter returned, she had one baby. The next time she returned, she was divorced and had two youngsters. The Bonel's son also freely moved in and out of their home between jobs. But the Bonels' didn't know how to tell their grown children that they really didn't feel it was right for them to move in without paying room and board. The only thing they could think of was to move into a one-bedroom home, and subtly tell their kids there was no room for them. They subsequently sold their medium-priced, large home and bought an elegant, one-bedroom house. Now the grown children and grandchildren come to visit, but they can't move in again since there aren't any extra bedrooms. Looking at this as an objective observer, you might think the Bonel's over-reacted a little, and that a simple heart-to-heart talk with their children could have saved them their large home. Yet, they're happy with their choice and their new home.

Following is an example in direct contrast to the Bonel's, who felt that they should have been getting room and board, but didn't know how to ask for it. Mr. and Mrs. Erickson didn't want room and board, and said so. But Ron, a nester who is a college graduate working full-time as an engineer, wanted to contribute. Mrs. Erickson refused his offer, reasoning that she and Dad didn't see the need for the extra money, and were just glad to have their son back home after college. It sounds almost too good to be true for Ron, but let's take a closer look.

Some parents want their adult children to live with them so much that they won't let them pay room and board. They say they merely want to do something for their children, that they have the room, and so on. They also may say they do not need the money. But could there be more to it than that? Could it be that these parents don't want to accept room and board because they want — perhaps subconsciously — to keep their relationship on the parent-child plateau? With this arrangement, the parents are seemingly still in control; they can continue to tell their children what to do. By accepting room and board, they would have to treat the nester as an adult. And that's something to think about! One mother who refuses rent from her daughter, a 24-year-old sales representative, states, "I am determined that things in this house should be the way my husband and I want them."[4]

Checking Accounts

Oftentimes, an adolescent's first use of bank services is a savings account. Then, when he has to start paying out money, he starts a checking account. Later on, if he needs a loan, it is only natural that he approach his own bank first to ask for financial assistance. Even though he has no prior credit rating, he has a definite advantage if the bank records indicate that he had handled a checking account without incurring overdrafts or bouncing checks. Since proper handling of a checking account indicates financial responsibility, and since banks feel an obligation to accommodate the legitimate credit needs of their depositors, the responsible nester might get the loan he seeks.

Most people use checking accounts to pay bills by mail and to pay for purchases as needed. It is certainly easier and safer than carrying cash around. Unfortunately, however, many young people have trouble making sure that they don't overdraw the account. Columnist Erma Bombeck wrote that one of her children wrote the bank a check to cover an overdraft! In addition, many young people have trouble keeping track of cancelled checks. One nester, Roy, is a good example.

Roy regularly asked his mother to get him money orders for his car payment, insurance, and charge card payments. Finally she suggested that Roy open up a checking account for paying his bills. This he did. Months went by, and one day his mom asked Roy how his checking account was working out. "Oh, I don't know," he answered. "I just write checks and then the bank sends them back to me. I've got them saved in my dresser drawer. What am I supposed to do with them now?" Mom told Roy that he should check his bank statement to see that neither he, nor the bank, had made any errors. Later that week, Roy spread his checking account papers all over the dining room table and worked for several baffling hours comparing the cancelled checks with his own records and the bank's statements. He finally gave up in defeat. But a good night's sleep gave him new encouragement, and he tackled the pile of papers again the following evening. At length, he told his mom that he was only off a couple of dollars and that he wasn't "gonna worry about that little bit!" Despite this imprecise approach to his checking balance, Roy learned a lot through this process.

After this checking account struggle, Roy could probably empathize with another nester, whose mother wrote that when she was sorting laundry some white breath mints rolled out. There were some numbers on one of them. It read, '2376-185.' When she asked her son if it was important, he said, that it meant either check no. 2376 for $1.85 or check no. 185 for $23.76. "Then he shrugged and popped it in his mouth."[5]

Taxes

If a person, even a nester, doesn't file income tax returns, he is going to be in trouble with the Internal Revenue Service sooner or later! So how is the young person going to learn about the world of taxes? There really isn't too much printed information available. And what is convenient is usually so involved and detailed that young people (and older ones, too!) can't or won't read it. So, like it or not, our nesters need to learn about the importance of collecting data and how and when to file from us, their parents, or from their friends.

But it's not always easy. Ann, a 24-year-old nester, is one of many people who have difficulty in handling personal mail. She will occasionally look over her mail pile after work, but unless something looks exceptionally interesting — like an invitation to a party — it just lies there on the table, begging to be taken care of. Or, sometimes she picks up her mail, walks to another part of the house where she casually opens the envelope, glances over its contents, and then drops it on the nearest table. With a person like Ann, it's almost predictable that when it's time for her to file her income tax forms with the IRS, she is going to have trouble finding her W-2 form (which comes in the mail during January to anyone who has earned income the preceding year). A gentle hint from Mom on the day the W-2 arrives, to the effect that Ann will need this form to do her income tax returns, may help in preventing a problem at a future date.

There's another tax complication that some nesters, and parents, need to be aware of: tax money is not withheld from the paycheck in certain jobs. It's true for anyone who is a sole proprietor of a business, for some salesmen and in some household and farm jobs, to name a few. In these cases, nesters should keep accurate records throughout the year so that the figures are available when the time comes to fill out the IRS return. However, it may be necessary to file

estimated tax returns four times a year in some of these jobs.
So, it might be advisable to check with an accountant or
CPA (certified public accountant) regarding one's taxes.

Parents can also be helpful to their nester at the time they
are working on their own IRS returns. It would be a
kindness to show their nester how the process is done, so
that he can be reminded to start compiling his data for Uncle
Sam. While it is appropriate for parents to remind their
nester — especially in his first year of paying taxes — it is
best for the nester to gather his own data and fill out the
form himself. Or, he could also take it to a professional tax
accountant and pay the fee, but it should be stressed that he
must allow plenty of time for professional help. Whatever
he chooses to do, however, the April 15th deadline may need
to be emphasized. By being responsible for his own taxes, he
will learn the mechanics and the cost of this necessary fact of
life. He must know that there will be a penalty from the
government if tax returns are not filed on time. An added
incentive is the possibility of getting an early refund if the
forms are sent in before the rush. If the forms are not sent in,
the government will keep the money that is withheld from
his paycheck to cover the taxes.

Despite the threat of being called nags, parents should
alert their nesters to the procedure until they get the hang of
it. It's a vital part of their financial education.

Budgeting

A good budget is helpful in reaching goals, and in
planning for emergencies. For example, here are three types
of goals. A nester's long-range goal could include saving
enough money for a down payment on a house, which
would take years to do. An intermediate goal would be
saving for a good suit, which might take several months to
acquire. Immediate goals would include items like rent, car
payment, insurance payments, etc. that have to be paid each
month.

*Patching the roof and painting the house are the obligations
of all sharing the same house.*

Not all people have the discipline to save and spend money wisely, however. Many people's first reaction to their financial situation is similar to Gary's, a 32-year-old nester. "The problem with my finances is that I just don't make enough money." Yet, when we look around at young people who are making their salaries stretch, we know almost without asking that they have the ability to save a little bit out of each paycheck. For them, then, it is not the amount of money that they have at their disposal that makes them successful, but the proper allocation of its spending.

One nester who hasn't learned this truism yet is Gary. He periodically moves in and out of his parents' home because he can't seem to make it on his own financially. However, if he could learn the secret of budgeting, he would probably be able to become financially independent from his folks.

Gary, like other grown kids, should determine his goals (long-range, intermediate, and immediate). A certain amount should be allocated for emergencies. Studies have shown that all successful people make lists — lists of daily chores, lists of yearly goals, lists of life goals. Money matters are no different. Encourage the nester to write down his income. Then he should itemize all his expenses for a month's time and decide which items should receive priority. Then he needs to ask himself how much he would be able to save and what he could do without.

One advantage of a balanced budget, where outflow does not exceed income, is that goals can be realized! He *can* get that car, or make that down payment on a house! "In three years since he moved into his parents' Miami house, one 24-year-old rock-music reporter has stashed away $6,000, bought a used car with cash, and traveled to England on his $12,800 salary. His room and board is $15 per week."[6]

A budget that is not in balance means that expenses are more than income, and this means that some goals will not be realized. For a nester this may mean a continued dependence on his parents.

Here are five simple budget rules that are easy to understand:

1. Write down goals, current expenditures, and
    estimated savings needed for intermediate and future
    goals.
2. Write down income.
3. Balance outgo with income.
4. Keep careful records of outgo and income.
5. Look over records periodically to make sure that
    spending is kept within budget.

Loans

Parents often run into the situation of a nester who needs
some extra cash, and the question keeps arising: is it a good
idea for parents to help out? Perhaps not always. But
sometimes it may be the only way for a young person, who
hasn't been working and purchasing long enough to
establish a credit rating, to get ahead financially. Let's look
at the pros and cons of loaning money to our nesters.

Twenty-year-old Jerry wanted to buy a used car. It was
seven years old, in good condition, and cost $1,800. His
folks could easily have lent Jerry the money, but they felt
that this was a good opportunity for him to learn how banks
operate, and to establish some credit. So they advised Jerry
to go to the bank for a car loan. This he did and was told he
would need a co-signer on the note. His parents agreed to
co-sign, making sure, however, that Jerry knew that this was
his loan and *he* would be responsible for paying it back. This
way, his parents were able to help him out financially,
without having to shell out the cash. Before you do this, be
sure you trust your child in financial matters, since a poor
payment record would reflect on your record.

Here's an example of a parent who did decide to shell out
cold, hard cash. Cheryl, at 25, wanted to buy into a
partnership with her two friends. The three women planned
to open up a specialty shop and needed money to buy
inventory. The shop would be in a good location, where
there was a need in the neighborhood for a business of this

type. It was also evident that they were taking a very business-like approach to the venture, for they had done a market analysis. Cheryl didn't have the capital for her share, so she approached her dad. He thought it was a great opportunity for his daughter, and since he had some cash reserves, he was willing to lend her the money she needed. He felt that it would be a good investment, one likely to succeed, and he could see that Cheryl was excited and enthusiastic about the business. So, he loaned her $6,000. They signed a formal agreement, specifying all the terms of the loan, including the repayment schedule and the interest rate. Cheryl's dad believes that ultimately his initial investment will be recouped, with interest. As an added plus, his daughter will make her debut into the business world.

As a caution, you may want to be familiar with Mrs. Bauer, which will portray the con of this issue. Mrs. Bauer and her husband, while he was alive, planned their finances so that they would have a good income upon retirement. However, Mr. Bauer died an untimely death at age 58 from a heart attack. So, in addition to their savings, Mrs. Bauer also had her husband's life insurance benefits, which were considerable. It appeared that she would have no financial problems in store for her. However, within a short time, actually before the second anniversary of his dad's death, her 28-year-old son, Mark, who was living with Mrs. Bauer, came to her with a sure-fire investment scheme. All he would need would be a temporary loan from his mother — a very hefty one though — and he would be able to increase the capital, pay his mother back and be off like a rocket. His enthusiasm completely flattened any questions his mother was able to muster, and over the objections of legal counsel, she made the loan her son requested. Within nine months it became evident that he would not make the financial killing he had envisioned, and before the year was out, his mother knew that she would never see her money again. This was doubly tragic because not only was his mother without funds (she lost the family home and had to go to work in a department store), but the four other children in the family lost their inheritance.

Many business ventures of a similar nature are quite risky despite market surveys and the enthusiasm of partners. So, parents should be very cautious about this type of loan, realizing the risk involved. In the event of a business failure and the inability of the nester to repay the loan, a lifetime of bitterness could follow. Points for a parent to consider before making a loan are:

1. Do the business partners have any managerial ability and experience?
2. In case of a joint venture, do partners know that they are *personally* responsible for partnership debts?
3. Have they made realistic sales projections that indicate an adequate profit?
4. Have they made arrangements for adequate accounting and tax matters?
5. In the event that one of the partners wants to leave the partnership, has a formula been agreed upon as to the amount to be paid by the remaining partners and the method and terms of payment?

Sometimes the desire of parents to help their offspring blinds them to the risk involved. Unfortunately, too much animosity has developed between relatives or friends whose joint ventures went awry. Yet, if after taking everything into consideration, you still want to loan the money to your nester, more power to you!

Some parents stated various reasons why they have loaned their nesters money. One mother wrote that her 23-year-old daughter "occasionally needs a loan for a payment that she is behind in—sometimes for a car payment and sometimes for an insurance payment." A 19-year-old male nester writes that he needs "loans—not gifts—for my social life and clothes." Another parent relates that her two grown sons have needed loans five times, in amounts of $3,000 or less, for trailer home investment, car purchases, etc. These loans are expected to be paid back as soon as possible. Yet another mother tells us of her 28-year-old daughter who lives at home and is working full time. "She needs $20 every other month for incidentals until her paycheck comes."

Health Insurance

Most people consider health insurance a necessity, but what 21-year-old knows or believes that? They still have that wonderful sense of invulnerability. So, often your nester needs to be educated about health insurance. Here is the story of one nester who had to learn the hard way.

Tony, now 21, is a nester who has never left home. He is now working for a small firm which doesn't have a group health insurance plan. After Tony left school he was no longer eligible for the family insurance plan that his father carried through his office. So, naturally mom and dad had suggested to Tony several times that he should get some health insurance coverage. All he would need, they suggested, would be a major medical plan, which shouldn't be too expensive for a healthy young man. They felt he really should be covered in case he was in an accident or came down with a costly illness. But, Tony didn't want to spend money on something so "non-essential" (in his words) as health insurance.

But, lo and behold, the day came when Tony told his mom that he could no longer stand the headaches he'd been having (these were news to mom) and that he was going to go to the doctor. It turned out to be nothing serious, but his trip to the doctor added impetus to mom's encouragement that he get health insurance. So, the next day, when his mom suggested that Tony find an insurance agent, he did. Within a week, he had an insurance policy.

The following month, when it was time to make his second monthly payment on the policy, Tony wrote the policy number on his check and mailed it in, but without the tear-off section of the policy notice that is supposed to be returned along with the check. He did the same thing the next month. Then he received a letter saying that the insurance company was cancelling him out because of non-payment. They had cashed his checks, but because he had neglected to return the stub, even though the policy number was written on Tony's check, his account had not been credited. Tony had to go back to his agent, retrieve his cancelled checks, and make copies of them in order to prove that he had made his premium payments. Tony learned that while it's important to have health insurance, it's also important to pay attention to the directions on the bill — any bill.

Conclusion

In dealing with money matters, we must consider what is best for all parties involved — the nester and the parents. Each should ask: What can I do? What am I willing to do? To answer these questions, one should honestly assess his feelings and then be open and frank with the others about these feelings. Would it be best to give financial aid freely, with no worry of payback? Would it be better to lend money with the expectation of being paid back on schedule? Or would a bank loan (with possibly the parents co-signing) be better? Each situation is going to be different and must be dealt with separately, carefully, and caringly.

In general, however, the conclusion can be drawn that it seems best for a nester who has some income to pay a percentage of it to his folks as room and board. If the situation is one where there is no income, or where the nester is saving money, perhaps some work arrangement can be made as a substitute for a monetary contribution.

Parents are responsible for the financial training of their children. Likewise, adult children should be committed to growing in financial responsibility. It's a two-way street.

Through loving concern and communication, most money problems and situations can be worked out in a positive way.

*"Aren't we a little embarrassed by what the neighbors will think
if our kids come home and live with us after college?
I mean, if we're such hot parents, and if our kids are so talented,
how come they're sleeping upstairs and eating
our peanut butter sandwiches?....
There's an attitude that a parent doesn't get the trophy
until they're out on their own."*
—Television host Phil Donahue.[1]

CHAPTER VII

Negative Attitudes

Having a nester in the home invites a lot of negative criticisms from our friends, our families, and even from ourselves. We need to recognize how these attitudes influence our actions, so we can relate to our nesters in a positive way.

The opinion of our friends, though subtle, can certainly influence our feelings and thus our actions — especially when we're not quite sure that what we're doing is the right thing. If the pressure of our friends' opinions is too strong, then we need to be aware of the kinds of negative feelings we're up against.

On the whole, it appears that society is not prepared to accept nesting, so we shouldn't be surprised when friends or neighbors make disparaging remarks about the practice. In our day and age, the emphasis is on individual success, and some members of society aren't really ready to view a nester as a success. Some parents have the impression that other people consider their offspring failures because they aren't living outside the family home.

Friends' Comments

The following comments from friends and family (as related in our survey) are typical:

- "If you're such great parents, your kids should be independently successful—not still living with you at home." (Some people think one has to leave home in order to be considered successful. Does this mean that a 50-year-old person who has had a successful career, but lives at home, is still considered unsuccessful?)

- "Isn't your kid sponging off you? How can you put up with him at home? These grown kids should be able to stand on their own two feet!" (You and your nester are the only ones who can determine whether he is sponging off you or really needs you.)

- "When you leave home, then we'll think of you as an adult, but not before, because when you're out on your own, you'll be forced to take care of yourself and you'll finally really be an adult!" (If this nester paid room and board and helped with the household chores — in short, was a contributing member of the house — possibly his parents would think of him as an adult.)

- "You're spoiling your kid by letting him live at home and doing everything for him." (There is a difference between spoiling an offspring and fulfilling a need. Spoiling is when you do things for a person which he can do for himself, as opposed to fulfilling a valid need.)

- "These kids are never going to grow up if they continue to live at home." (Just because they live in the parental home doesn't mean that they won't grow and mature. Growth can take place wherever a person lives if he takes responsibility for himself and his actions.)

- "All 18-year-olds should be out of the home because twenty years ago we were out at that age." (Was everyone really out of the house at 18 then? Chances are that most people who say this, who did leave home at age 18, had to go through a lot of unnecessary loneliness and misguidance before actually becoming mature.)

- "When is she getting married and leaving home?" (This attitude may have come from Colonial times, as the following quote indicates:

  "A girl needed a husband for support, since there was scarcely any work open to her outside the house. The few women who remained without husbands in Colonial days were looked down on — it was agreed that something must be the matter with them and parents were likely to be embarrassed to have an unwed daughter on their hands.

Unmarried women of twenty-five were described as a 'dismal spectacle.'

"Unmarried men were not in much better repute. In Hartford, Connecticut, bachelors were taxed twenty shillings a week 'for the selfish luxury of solitary living.' They were expected to report periodically to a magistrate just to make sure they were behaving themselves. Puritan New England did not look kindly upon young marriageable males whiling away their time when they could be producing children. This was no place for sowing wild oats."[2]

Times have changed, and thankfully so, but still society has a bit of a hangover from these Colonial times, in that our first impression of an older, unmarried person is often questioning or negative. However, when we really stop to think about it, it's really a person's own business whether or not they choose to stay single.)

Responses to Friends' Comments

It may seem an impossible task to change our friends' attitudes. However, it *is* possible to deliberately choose how we will react. Following are ways that some families have responded to negative comments:

- **Accept them in silence and become resentful.** If we do accept these comments in silence, then emotions can fester and pop out in open resentment toward the nester with such remarks as, "Why don't you get a decent job that pays a living wage? Then my friends will quit bugging me about you!"

- **Get defensive.** "Where I live is none of your business!"

- **Ignore them.** "I get bad vibes from friends and relations about living at home, but I just pay no attention to them. If they don't like it, that's their problem, not mine."

- **Explain why they are a nesting family.** "He needs (or wants) to live at home for awhile. Anyway, the family should dictate to society, not vice versa."

- **Praise the benefits of nesting.** "When I hear disparaging remarks, I tell that person about the positive side of living at home."

If you are being exposed to negative attitudes, it's going to be harder to deal with nesting in your home. So, if you have a nester, the object is to learn to deal with the negativeness positively. Then you can accept and enjoy living together as a family.

The following comments are from people reacting positively to negative comments:

- "I feel this is a special time in our lives and I want to enjoy it."

- "I do what I see is right for our family."

- "I could move out, but there is no pressure from my parents to go. I'm glad that they let me live at home."

- "My daughter seems to appreciate all the things I did for her when she was young, because she is anxious to be helpful to me now that she's grown up."

- "If I can't get along with my parents, I won't be able to get along with other people who may have differing attitudes."

- "Occasionally our situation gets criticized, but it's mostly by people who don't understand family ties."

- "I tell my buddies to compare my bank account to theirs."

- "I tell them they're nuts to criticize because I have it so great."

- "I try not to worry about it when my friends make negative remarks."

- "Every family is different and every person is different. Let's live our own lives and let others live as they choose."

Parents' Attitudes

When parents feel negative attitudes from their friends about their young people nesting, then many of them begin to have negative feelings of their own as well. However, some parents themselves doubt the wisdom of their young people nesting, as the following comments show:

- "Whose house is this, anyway? Yours or mine?" (Some families with nesters have a problem with a confrontation of wills. We need to decide whether the nester is a guest, a boarder, or an integral part of the family whose wishes, needs, and desires are considered.)

- "Is this ever going to end? Is he ever going to move out or will he be living here for the rest of his life?" (Social attitudes about staying home are so negative that anyone contemplating that choice could have cause for concern.)

- "Years ago young people were blamed for the deterioration of the family because they left home. Now when they need to return to

that home, some people feel they cannot stand on their own feet."
(It looks like no matter what young people do — stay or leave —
they will be criticized.)

- "I'm a failure as a parent because my kid is a failure." (The
nester doesn't have a big-salaried job, can't afford to live in an
apartment, and so he has to live at home.)

- "I know what's good for you better than you do." (Some
parents have an attitude of infinite wisdom regarding their nester.
This attitude can ultimately stifle them.)

Nesters' Attitude

Some nesters' own attitudes prevent them from nesting
when it really would be better for them to do so.

- "I need to live at home because I can't afford to continue on
with school if I have to pay high rent and tuition too. But I can't go
back home because I bragged when I moved out that I could be a
big success on my own." (Hurt pride and stubbornness can prevent
a nester from rejoining the family in time of need.)

The end result of negative comments from ourselves or
thoughtless friends is that we take out our irritations on our
nester, spouse, or other children. Or we bury the remark
deep within, where it festers, only to emerge later as a
stinging comment to some unsuspecting family member.
Negative comments may affect a parent or nester so deeply
that the nester is no longer able to live on at home.

A nester's underlying attitude toward home, parents, and
family will certainly dictate his or her actions. Therefore, it
will be helpful to look at situations where nesting has
worked out well, and examine the nester's attitude.

One 22-year-old nesting son writes, "I'm glad that they
(my parents) let me live at home. I don't wish to move out.
I'm financially able, but there is no pressure from my
parents to go. I brag to my friends how wonderful and
understanding my folks are. We don't have any troubles."
Maybe the key word in this son's writing is "let." He realizes
that his parents are allowing him to live there; it's a privilege
that he appreciates.

One young lady said she felt that it was important to know that she was welcome to live in her parents' home. She declined, feeling it wouldn't work out, but it meant a great deal to her that her parents voiced their willingness to have her live with them if she ever wanted or needed to do so.

Another young woman gave this heartfelt statement, "Be it ever so humble, there's no place like my Mom's!"

Sometimes it's not easy for the nester to fit into the daily routine in his parents' home, now that he is an adult. Kate, quoted in *Time* magazine, realistically states, "I have learned the hard way not to fight with them (her parents) about my sense of values. I now realize I have to compromise. This is their territory."[3]

A young lady, age 22, wrote, "I am appreciative of the fact that I can live at home while getting started in a career. However, my need to grow and be more independent will affect the current living arrangements in a short time. I plan to move soon."

The following two nesters show a wide degree of variance in attitudes:

A 31-year-old female nester wrote, "I'm very happy with the situation. It seems to be a good one. Financially, it's affordable for me and a little extra money for my parents. In terms of personal growth, it's providing an opportunity for furthering my education." (She's working on her master's degree.)

On the other hand, some nesters feel guilty about living at home. Like so many others, they think they shouldn't still be living with their parents. One 32-year-old nester, in particular, has lived at home with his parents for many years and evidently it's worked out well for both him and his family. Yet, he feels guilty about living at home. It could be that societal pressure has affected this nester's attitude.

Author's note: Research makes it apparent that there are difficulties in living with a nester because of social attitudes. But if these difficulties are faced and dealt with, then nesting can be a workable situation. Clearly, what nesting families are asking for is a non-judgmental attitude from society, so that they can feel free to live as they feel they must. Certainly it is more helpful to try to understand other people than it is to criticize them. Nesting has occurred throughout the centuries, and history will ultimately judge how good or how bad an idea it is.

Target Departure Date

It is much easier to have patience with a live-in situation if one knows that there is a termination date. Yet, only a few families say that they have discussed an expected departure date, such as a wedding, a college entrance, or a specific arbitrary target date for the nester to move. One mother wrote that her nester was planning to leave after he finished school (he was commuting to college while living at home), for then he would be able to support himself.

Some families said that they had "vaguely" discussed the topic, and one nester wrote that his family had discussed a "tentative" departure time. One mother mentioned that her nester planned to leave home when the weather was suitable for a move. One weary mother of nine children (two of them nesters) wrote, "Yes, I have discussed it with them, and I told them anytime was fine with me!!!"

However, some families felt that length of stay wasn't a problem:

- "They all leave on their own naturally when it's time. It just isn't this daughter's time yet, I guess. I don't understand attitudes of people today. They think when kids get out of high school they have to leave home. Why? In order to be independent? They can be independent and still live at home."

- "I feel if you raise your child right, there's never any time you're going to have to say, 'You have to leave' because they'll know when it's time to leave."

- "Surely the average young adult wants to become independent just as soon as he is able and will leave the family home when his need (whether financial or emotional) is fulfilled."

- "He won't be with us forever — it won't be for much longer."

- "My parents always let us know the door was open, and that we could come home. But they also let us know that it (our stay) was temporary."

Some parents felt nesting was acceptable for a limited time only, but after that time it was no longer acceptable. One mother with a 30-year-old son living at home said, "I think after a certain age it's better for everyone for the offspring to have his own apartment." Two other parents were a little more specific:

"It's okay for them to live at home, but if carried out into the mid-twenties or so, it's too extreme."

"By age 25 I feel they should be out and on their own."

So, some people think that it's all right to nest for a period of time, but that it shouldn't be too long. How long is too

Children need the respect of their parents even when they make choices different from those their parents feel are right.

long? It's up to the individual families themselves to decide, without influence from friends or relations. It would seem that a discussion of plans with a specific or tentative moving date would ease tensions. This would help provide parents with patience and make life with a nester a more pleasant experience.

CHAPTER VIII

Some Nesters Choose a Lifestyle Different from Their Parents'

Just what is considered an alternate lifestyle? In one family it may be smoking cigarettes and in another it may be involvement in hard drugs. Some parents react as intensely to the first as another family would to the second. One father kicked his son out of the family home because of his use of hard drugs and another father kicked his daughter out of the home because she didn't leave home for Sunday church service on time.

It is important to realize that it's not always the severity of the action, but the depth of the family's feeling toward that action, that triggers a response. Parental feelings can intensify a problem between parents and nester and make it more difficult to solve. When parents are confronted with a nester who has chosen a life with a different set of values than theirs, the parents usually have difficulties dealing with the situation. They can become perplexed and frozen into inaction because they are unsure of the proper course of action.

...parents may well be tempted to think that the end of all things is at hand [when offspring choose an alternative lifestyle]. They are likely to be sure when young people "drop out," scorning the traditional work ethic to live in self-imposed indolent poverty, or when they live in coed college dorms and bring home opposite-sex friends on weekends expecting to share the same bedroom with them. Understating things somewhat, sociologist Robert Winch remarks that "This is one helluva time to be a parent."[2]

141

Society Affects Our Values

Societal norms can affect us deeply, sometimes causing us to change our individual values. This may be for the good, since it may make life easier. We might also be adversely affected and our life made more difficult.

> Yet no matter how tightly the family draws in on itself, the outer world cannot be kept out. It follows the family into the home. Television, radio, books, magazines and newspapers now subject adults and children alike to a flood of external ideas. Most of this broadening of outlook improves the quality of life; it has made people better informed and more sophisticated than ever before. But this great benefit is not achieved without cost. For the mass media's flood of information also transmits the stresses and conflicting attitudes of the outer world into the heart and mind of the family, challenging and often upsetting values.[3]

Some parents give up. Other parents rant and rave. What are parents to do? Their nester may have a different set of sexual values and may insist that, while living at home or during a visit, he have sleeping arrangements of which his parents disapprove. In situations like this, needless to say, parents are thrust into uncomfortable predicaments. But, it's also difficult for the young people, as the next quote illustrates.

> "I wasn't really nervous about meeting Cindy's mother," says Nick. "It was her father that scared me. After all, I was sleeping with his daughter; I could almost feel the shotgun in my back."[4]

One nester on the Phil Donahue Show was having a problem with her mother.

> "I'm twenty-five years old. I've been married and divorced. When I was married, my husband and I lived with my mom. Now I still live at home. But I'm having a discrepancy with my mother on who to bring into the house and who to bring into certain parts of the house."[5]

And on it goes. Because of rapidly changing societal values, families are caught in the middle with no firm guidelines as to how to act. But, keeping the perspective that love and respect for each other is a fundamental base for our adult-to-adult relationships, it will be easier to explore this topic and come to a workable decision.

Parental Love and Respect

Can parents still love and respect a nester if he chooses a lifestyle not in keeping with theirs? Many parents have wrestled with the knotty problem of how to maintain open communication between themselves and their adult offspring when this happens. Vicky, a mother of seventeen children, says she doesn't want to lay too much guilt on her children. However, she tells herself that if they end up with different values, she might cry for a while, but she won't die over it.[6] That's an advisable attitude to take. It's so easy to think the end of the world has come if our grown children depart from our norms.

We can more easily accept such deviations in other families than in our own family. It might help if we look at our children through the eyes of an outsider.

We all know families in which the offspring have chosen to use marijuana and family relations still continue — life still goes on. Another point to consider if we're upset is *why* we are upset. Do we fear criticism from our friends, or are we truly concerned about our nesters? Our relationship with our own offspring is much more important than any we can have with our friends.

Counselor Ralph Ranieri feels that grown sons and daughters "must respect their parents' feelings and customs, but they must also feel free to make legitimate choices that may be contrary to their parents' aspirations."[7]

First, parents have to sort out in their own minds just how to relate to an offspring who has branched out beyond their values. How does one go about that sorting? How can we still respect someone if we don't approve of his conduct? Psychologist Howard Halpern gives some insight regarding this:

> The child thinks he has done something unthinkable, beyond the pale. His punishment for deeply disappointing the parents is not the withdrawal of love, but the withdrawal of their *respect*. The granting and withdrawal of respect are enormously powerful enforcers. We need to feel that our parents value us as worthwhile

human beings, and do not simply love us because we are theirs. We need to feel our parents *like* us. Parents communicate that if we don't follow their rules, they may still love us, because after all, as parents they *should*, but they won't *like* us. And that's heavy.[8]

But still, how can we *respect* our nester if he has chosen a different set of values than those in which we believe? Halpern gives some further suggestions. Speaking from an offspring's viewpoint, he says:

> You have to indicate your discovery (to your parents) that different ways of being, which your parent may have invalidated as the practice of sinners or barbarians, have value in the lives of others because others, like you, are different from him or her. You have to make it clear that you have no desire to have them change the rules they live by because that is what seems right to them. Neither do you need their approval of your choices. What you would really like is for them to maintain their respect even when you make choices different from those they feel are right....[9]

There are just so many more pressures on young people today than we parents experienced in our growing-up years; pressures such as:

- Enjoy sexual freedom
- Resist authority
- Drink a 6 pack of beer
- Take a six-month leave from life
- Smoke a joint of pot

In thinking about it realistically, how can we expect our young people to react to situations as we once did when they are living under different social pressures than we experienced? We have to give our adult children credit for examining an issue, and making the best decision that they can under the existing restrictions they experience. Then, it becomes their decision. And true, their decision may be different from one we as parents would have made when we were their age. But again, they are living under different conditions than we were. Society is much more open and accepting than it was twenty years ago. Can't we respect our nesters for having examined the situation and come to a decision without making a judgment against them?

If a parent feels that his nester's behavior is improper or definitely wrong, he has a right and a responsibility to convey this to his nester. The parent must make it clear, though, that it's the *behavior* he objects to — not the nester. Some nesters make the following plea,

"You and I are different, and I respect who you are and would like you to respect who I am."[10]

If our nester has made choices that are working to help him live a fuller, happier life, then the end result is that he's making choices that are good for him.[11] For example, Ted, at 21-year-old student, felt he needed to retire for several months and think about the direction his life was headed. After this sojourn — which appeared to be sheer laziness to his parents — he decided to change his major. Now he is studying in earnest and is looking forward to graduating and then working in his chosen field.

Parental Standards

Some parents have clearly announced their standards so that their nester knows what's acceptable in the home. Even while loving and respecting a nester who lives a different lifestyle, parents can still have house standards. As one mother of a 31-year-old nesting son stated, "This is our house. You are welcome here, but this is what we believe in and that governs what goes on in this house." Parents have different flash points — differing levels where they draw the line — and each nester should know where his parent draws the line on a particular issue. The following nester who telephoned into the show received some free advice from television host Phil Donahue.

Mr. Donahue: "So you want freedom to bring a girlfriend home?"

Young man: "Yeah, I do, because the lease where we're living is under both of our names (my mother's name and mine)."

Mr. Donahue: "Oh, OK, you want to be able to sleep with this girl?"

Young man: "Pardon me?"

Mr. Donahue: "You want to be able to sleep with her."

Young man: "I want to be able to have the same freedom I'd have if I were on my own."

Mr. Donahue: "So, you want to be able to sleep with her?"

Young man: "Right."

Mr. Donahue: "Is that right?"

Young man: "That's right."

Mr. Donahue: "All night long? Don't you feel any obligation to at least honor your mother's traditional values?"

Young man: "But I'm honoring her traditional value by paying half of the rent!"

Panel Member: "But you're living under her roof."

Young man: "I think I'm honoring it by..."

Mr. Donahue: "Hang on just a moment. I've got some free advice for you. Go out and pay all your rent and sleep with her but don't do it in your mother's house."[12]

Following is an example of a young person who did move out because of her mother's objections. Tracey, a young female guest on the Phil Donahue Show, said: "When I was nineteen years old, I had a boyfriend my mother didn't care for and she gave me a choice. Either stay home and get rid of him, or you can leave and have him. So, I left home. Well, he went away to school right after I moved out of the house. So, I turned right around and moved back home."[13]

The point that needs to be made here is that the parents are in charge. It's their house, and they set the standards for the house. If these offspring do not agree with these standards, they are free to move out.

Specific Topics

In talking and communicating with other families about cigarettes, marijuana and hard drugs, alcohol, and sex, the responses were interesting.

Cigarettes. The responses about cigarette smoking were surprising. Only about a quarter of the nesters smoked cigarettes. One nester even wrote, "No, I don't smoke cigarettes! Do I look dumb?" One mother wrote that her nester did smoke, but that he had been asked not to smoke in the home. The mother said she worried because they have a "No Smokers" Household Insurance policy.

Smoking was not a problem in some of these homes because other family members also smoked and it was an accepted thing to do. But in other homes it was bothersome to the non-smokers. One mother reported that she felt smoking was distasteful to other family members, and that it set a bad example for younger siblings. However, her nesters were permitted to smoke in the home. They didn't ask permission and apparently it never occurred to her that she could refuse to let them smoke in the home.

Some parents placed restrictions on the smoking. One father stated that his son could only smoke upstairs in his bedroom. Another nester said that when she wanted a cigarette, she had to smoke outside on the front porch.

Reactions to nesters smoking varied from mild to intense. One mother said it was bothersome, and another replied that she and other family members strongly disliked the nester's smoking. Another mother said that she permits her nester to smoke in the home, but that she found it very irritating. An important point to bear in mind is that the depth of the family members' feelings should be taken into account, and that there should be open discussion about the topic if it's causing disruption or irritation in the family. Rather than let these feelings of irritation fester, it's best to talk them out and set some house rules regarding smoking.

In one family there was quite a role reversal — the mother smoked and the nesting daughter didn't like it. Mother wrote, "I smoke, she does not. I'm sure she'd prefer that I not smoke, but I feel it's my house and I'm entitled to more or less do my own thing." If the adult daughter doesn't like to live with a smoker, she can move out.

Marijuana and Hard Drugs. In spite of the fact of the illegality of drugs, many people still wanted to communicate their feelings about marijuana and hard drugs. Most parents said that there was no use of drugs by their nesters, several said it was questionable, and some replied in the affirmative.

As might be expected, emotions were definitely intense in response to this question. One mother wrote, "When our son was arrested for selling, we nearly died. My husband is a prominent person in our community. People felt sorry for us. Three of our friends came over and asked if they could help us with either money or just friendly support. This meant so very much to us. Other friends hurt us deeply by their condemning attitude. We never did talk about it with our relatives, except some close ones. We made our son work two jobs all summer to pay off the lawyer. He also worked for free for us on Saturdays. He's on probation for a long time. It's been very hard on the family."

Another mother stated that her two older children had been involved with hard drugs. The younger children have seen the resulting pain and harm to family relationships, friends, jobs, and health. They have said that they aren't going to follow their older brother and sister's lead.

Other reactions to this problem were:

- "Yes, I use pot," says one nester, "but my parents aren't thrilled about it...."

- "I would assume that she uses drugs," wrote a mother. "As far as I know, it has not affected any other family members. If drugs are really being used, I would guess the younger children know it."

- "Possibly he uses drugs. That might account for the behavior changes that I notice and which definitely have affected other family members."

- "Yes, he uses drugs. The rest of the family thinks he's a bum."

- "Yes, she's used them in the past. I don't know the extent. Everyone knows it hasn't been for the best."

If a nester uses marijuana or hard drugs, it generally affects the other family members. Then the family has to decide how to handle this situation. And handle it they should. Ignoring the situation won't make it go away.

Alcohol. Parental responses regarding alcohol showed that about three quarters of the nesters do imbibe. For some of the families where nesters do drink alcohol, this is not a problem, because, as with cigarettes, other family members do likewise. Some families share wine or beer at family meals in common. However, as with cigarette usage, whether moderate or abusive, this could cause problems depending upon how the families react.

Some parents felt drinking alcohol was a bad example to younger siblings. Other parents worried about a nester having a car accident when driving while drinking. One mother was concerned about drinking because all her children have an extremely low tolerance for alcohol. One nester wrote that yes, he drank and, yes, his parents worried, but that they did trust his judgment in not abusing alcohol. Another parent wrote that her nester's drinking caused tension in the home. And yet a third parent wrote that both her nesters drank beer. She personally felt that it was the same kind of a drug as marijuana, in that the affects of their use were similar.

A nester wrote, "I use it (alcohol), *not* abuse it, therefore my family need not worry." The parents of this nester are happy that he never has abused alcohol. Still, they do have some concern about him in this regard. A person's driving ability is certainly impaired after a few beers. And, this nester stops at the local bar every Friday afternoon with the rest of the fellows on his crew.

Sex. Most parents have heard the wail, "But everyone's doing it!" Well, families I communicated with indicated otherwise. A little less than a quarter of the nesters themselves or their parents indicated an involvement on the part of the nester in sexual activity, while a little less than half replied negatively. The rest were unaware of their nesters' sexual activities or preferred not to respond to this topic.

One writer felt that if parents demonstrated affection more openly with their children and their mate, and tried to

understand the pressure for sex from their kids' point of
view, that some of the problems relating to premarital sex
could be alleviated. She writes:

> Affection: One reason sex has become such an explosive issue is
> that, despite all the talk, adults in America are quite reluctant to
> express affection openly. So sex becomes this big mystery that goes
> on someplace in secret.
>
> Now I don't advocate parents acting out sexually in front of
> children. Far from it!
>
> But I do know it is healthy and produces good attitudes to...hug
> your kids, kiss your mate. Show that mature adult affection is a
> wonderful thing, and sex is only part of it. This is the healthy
> context in which we want kids to see sex.[14]

One young man of 27 claimed no sexual involvement. "I
haven't met the right girl yet," he said. One mother replied
that she didn't know if her nester was involved in a sexual
relationship; she went on the say, "It's none of my business."

A young woman said that, yes, she had a sexual
relationship with her boyfriend, but that her parents didn't
know of it. "This is my life, my responsibility. Sex was/is
never discussed with my parents." Another nester replied
with a tongue-in-chek response to the question, "Does adult
offspring engage in sexual activity?" with, "Only when
offered." And yet another wrote, "Not at home."

The most difficult aspect of premarital sex for families
was when unmarried nesters wanted to engage in sex in their
parents homes even though it was against parental values.
In a very few cases, sexual relations of unmarried nesters
was not a problem because it was not against parental
values. One nester whose mother did not object replied that
"privacy is a problem occasionally — but it would be with
any roommate though."

Another problem was mentioned by a mother of two
nesters — a son and a daughter. Both were sexually active,
but it was only infrequently and discreetly for the son.
However, the daughter was sexually active often and with
no discretion. This was very hard for her parents to handle.
Another mother wrote that the family is aware that a nesting

son is sexually involved with his girlfriend and that it definitely embarasses the teens in the home, who believe it's wrong.

Conclusion

In conclusion, if nesters choose a lifestyle different than that of the parents, this can cause problems that should be dealt with frankly and openly. Perhaps these problems need to be discussed, clarifying for both parties the expectations each hold. Family love can still exist. Parents can still love *and* respect their nesters in spite of this difference in lifestyle. Respect of the other person can only come when there is an attitude of "I don't like what you do. Yet, I see you've chosen what you think is best for you, and I still accept you and like you as a person."

*"Parents of grown children tell me
their children don't need door keys anymore;
they need a revolving door.
They're in when they're
out of work, out of money, out of socks, out of food
and in debt.
They're out when they're
in love, in the bucks, in transit, in school,
and have outgrown their need for milk."*
—Columnist, Erma Bombeck

CHAPTER IX

Reroosting:
Returning Nesters

Not only are grown offspring *staying* in the family home, but many who had left are *returning*. More and more parents are seeing their homes fill up again — homes that they thought they had all to themselves because at one time their children had all grown and left. Parents are remodeling basements, garages, and spare bedrooms for these returning offspring. In a New York suburb so many families were illegally renovating their homes to accommodate married offspring with families, that the town finally made these two-family dwellings legal.[1]

Grown offspring all over the nation are returning home. One man in Massachusetts feels that even many of the college graduates in his town are returning home. "A businessman from heavily 'rerooted' Cambridge says, 'These are the children of academics who floated through school, majored in Renaissance literature, and find there

153

Just as one child "matures" and leaves home, another often returns home after finding out that a desired job pays too little to survive comfortably.

aren't any jobs for humanities students. They know a good deal when they see it — full refrigerator, a TV, a bed — and so home they come.' "[2]

However, it's not only college graduates, but students, working offspring, and out-of-work sons and daughters who are returning home.

Some returnees come home to re-establish ties with the family, as in the next two stories. One young man, after graduating from college, moved out of state and stayed away for five years. Then he decided to go on to law school; but before he did he wanted to spend several months at home. "It was important to me to get back in touch with them (my parents), to let them know what I was doing. I was about to live much farther away from home, to make a serious commitment to a career. It was just very important for me to make my family a part of that."[3]

One mother wrote of her returning daughter, "When she became engaged she moved back home eagerly and seemed to enjoy a renewal or reconciliation with the family. It was as if she realized that her rebellion during the early teen years had been ill-advised and finally she appreciated what had always been available to her. Since her marriage, she and her spouse have shown a need to visit both their families' homes, although they live in their own apartment. The family home seems to generate a much-needed sense of security and belonging."

It's a comforting, reassuring feeling for grown offspring to know that they're welcome at home. "...He or she wants parents there as a home base to return to in time of need. Even after moving out, it is important to feel there's a home to return to if the going gets tough."[4]

Disadvantages of Reroosting

Besides the obvious difficulty in learning how to live together again, there are often other disadvantages of returnees, especially recurrent returnees. The emotional upheaval can be draining to both parents and offspring. A neighbor related how painful it was for her when her son kept moving in and out. "I wept and wailed for weeks the first time my son moved out. I didn't cry nearly so long when he left the second time, and even less the third time.... Finally, the sixth time he moved out I said, 'You're not coming back, are you?' " It is also just plain hard work to keep continually moving furniture back and forth.

Continually moving grown children from one place to another was also hard on the following family. This family had just helped their 21-year-old son get settled into a house that he was sharing with three buddies. They were all starting another year at the university. But, just two weeks prior to that, the whole family had also helped an older daughter move from an apartment into a school dorm. Katie, their 15-year-old daughter, sighed, "When it's time for me to move in a couple of years, the family is going to be so tired of moving people that they won't want to help me!"

Another father said that his daughter was in the habit of moving often — sometimes as often as every two weeks. His family, too, was getting tired of all the moving. At some point the parents must put their foot down and say, "Enough is enough! Get settled some place and stay there for a while!"

One of the biggest disadvantages of having a returnee is that they bring all their stuff back home with them — boxes of books, stacks of furniture, racks of clothes, bikes and all kinds of recreational equipment, kitchen utensils, and linens. They want to keep it all safely stored away while they are rerooting. Then they can take it all with them again when they move the next time. The family is somehow expected to find room for it all. One newly married son built a section of shelves in his parents' basement to store wedding presents while he and his new bride lived abroad for a year.

Some things don't take much room, but they can be disturbing nonetheless. In the author's family, Pat, a college student who returned home for the summer, brought his pet, Zebineazer T. Regalo. Who was Zeb? His pet tarantula! Why the fancy name? "Well," he explained, "Zebineazer is his first name. He just looked like a Zeb. 'T.' stands for tarantula, and I chose 'Regalo' for his last name because that means 'present' in Spanish and he was a present from my buddies for Christmas. Simple, huh, Mom?" Some of the family members were quite upset at the thought of having a pet like that in the house!

The situation of a returnee has a different effect on the home than if the nester had just continued to live on after he reached 18. Fitting back into the daily family life after having experienced independent living usually is difficult. For example, the rerooosted nester, when he lived outside the parental home, had gotten used to freedom from parental supervision, not having to show consideration for other members of the family, being able to smoke in his own place, and being able to keep any hours he desired.

Parents, on the other hand, have become used to not having to worry about their grown offspring, and to having extra space and privacy in the family home, and not having to share the bathroom. "Long-awaited vacations or a move to a smaller, cheaper place may have to be postponed, and those who've enjoyed peace, quiet and exclusive bathrooms may shrink from the sudden invasion of privacy. Others fret over the diet and romantic activities of 22-year-olds as though they were 12 again. You find yourself listening at night for the car to come back, wondering if your son's okay."[5]

" 'It takes a group of very mature people to make it work,' says Ruth Neubauer, a marriage therapist in Yonkers, New York.... 'Old conflicts are awakened and many parents just carry on being parents, taking over the grandchildren and shaking their heads at new ideas. It's difficult to let children make their own mistakes when you are all under the same roof.' "[6]

It's not easy to assimilate grown children back into the

household. "The big problem...is that nobody quite knows what to expect and how to behave. Therefore all are proceeding with great caution, continually on the alert about each other's idiosyncrasies and needs, if only to avoid outright conflict."[7]

Other children in the family also have to make some adjustments in their lifestyle when an older sibling returns home. They again have to take phone messages (and get scolded if not taken properly), be ordered about by the rerooster, and probably share the bathroom again.

The following example illustrates the difficulty that can arise between a rerooster and a sibling. Jill, a 20-year-old rerooster, was having a loud, heated quarrel with Stan, her 17-year-old brother, about the family car. He had gotten a driver's license after Jill had moved out and enjoyed the use of the car. Now that she had returned home they were having problems with one more person sharing the car. Both of them wanted to use the car the following Friday night. Stan didn't want to fight, so he fled to the bathroom and locked the door. Jill wasn't finished with her tirade against him, so she followed him down the hall and hollered at him through the locked bathroom door. This got no response, so she kicked the door. She apparently kicked it harder than she thought or else the door, which was hollow, was more fragile than she realized — for she felt the toe of her thick-soled wooden shoe going right through the outer layer of the door!

While quick-to-anger Jill has a lot to learn about both compromise and communication, all nesting families have to learn a lot of things all over again when an adult offspring returns home. But in most families, points of conflict can be discussed, each one's priorities stated and a settlement negotiated.

One friend mentioned that her daughter had made an observation regarding reunited families. "Large families seem to have their most difficult children coming home while the achievers are doing just fine on their own." They seem to return because they have difficulty getting along with both family and the outside world. The old adage, "The more difficult it is to love an unlovable child, the more he needs that love," is very true! And home they come for it!

Advantages of Reroosting

The positive side of reroosting is that the nester generally has a new appreciation for the benefits of living at home. Hopefully, he no longer takes meals, laundry and cooking for granted. Once a grown child has been out of the home and on his own, he really appreciates having these things done for him...at least when he first returns! Also, parents can now view their nester as an adult a lot easier than if he had lived at home continuously. "When you've been on your own for a number of years and you and your parents have gone your separate ways (no matter how much you keep in touch), you begin to treat each other as adults."[8]

Mark Twain once remarked, "When I was a boy of fourteen, my father was so ignorant, I could hardly stand the old man around. But when I got to be twenty-one, I was astonished at how much he had learned in seven years." What a great quote to express how nesters/reroosters come around to seeing their folks as reasonable, and "neat" people. And while the young adult develops more respect for his parents, the process works to his benefit too. "Your independence is taken for granted at last, and you and your parents finally balance on the seesaw. 'It isn't a question merely of the young person's becoming independent,' says Tilla Vahanian, a New York psychotherapist. 'It is mutual, with both parents and children knowing how to establish the right distance.' "[9] During reroosting, parents and nester can start off on a new foot and gain a closer relationship (if parents can overlook certain drawbacks such as pet tarantulas!).

Another advantage of having a returnee is that, when he asks to move back, you have a perfect opportunity to lay down some rules.

Helen, a rerooster, said she appreciates having her very own phone-answering service now that she has returned home. Even if she is out of the house, there is generally someone around to take her messages. This was certainly not the case when she lived alone in an apartment.

A mother of a rerooster writes, "It's rewarding for us to see...how our son has matured, accepted responsibility, and become more aware of others.... It gives me a wonderful feeling to see him appreciate home more, and no longer take its comforts for granted.... He remarks, 'It's good to be here,' 'It felt good going to church with you,' or 'I'm sure glad the family went camping together this summer.' There were times during his high school years when peers, an important part of anyone's life, seemed to definitely overshadow family outings. He now appreciates his friends, parents, siblings, and parent's friends for what each has to offer."

The author's daughter, Maureen, who has been a rerooster, has a few comments about returning home. She says, "As I was leaving my parents home the first time (when I had a bedroom upstairs) my sisters were almost selling lottery tickets to see who would get my room. Thank goodness, though, I've never heard Ma and Pa say, 'No room at the inn' whenever I've said I wanted to come back home. But each time I move back home it gets a bit trickier. Once you leave, your spot is up for grabs. But you learn to be crafty. The third and last time I came back all the regular bedrooms were full, so I fashioned myself a spot in a corner of the recreation room. I had a couple of hazards to watch out for though. Between the pool cues and the arms of the foosball table, it was much like an obstacle course. The day started off by seeing if I could miss bumping my head on a foos arm or rolling over a cue stick as I got up out of the rollaway bed. This is not to mention the problem of where to dress, since there was no door on the rec room and two of my brothers had to walk through it to get to their bedroom. After I moved out again, my vacated spot in the rec room remained empty until my brother moved back from college, bringing his tarantula with him. No one wanted him for a roommate then because Zeb, his pet, took up a corner next to his bed!"

My husband and I have always welcomed guests into our home either for dinner or overnight. Possibly this practice made us open to the idea of sharing our roof with our adult children. The following two stories illustrate life with a full nest.

"I feel that my parents were able to accommodate us adult children at home," Maureen continues, "in part, because they had plenty of practice having other people staying at our home. Many times during my childhood our house was filled with strangers. At least, they were strangers to me. My folks have always had a soft spot for anyone who needed a place to stay. An example is Vicky, a friend of mine (my current away-from-home roommate). She had car problems last summer while I was back in the nest. Because she worked just down the road from my place of employment, I offered her a ride to work. For convenience, she stayed overnight. The night stretched into three weeks because she couldn't afford to get the car fixed right away. After about two weeks, my brother, Tom, finally noticed her frequency around the house. He asked Vicky, 'Have you moved in too?' At the same time we also had two cousins from Denver staying for several weeks. Also, our married brother and his wife had just moved out after a month stay between apartments."

The author's uncle, married but childless, has a favorite story about temporarily staying over at our house. Waking up one morning and wanting to use the bathroom, he listened to the hallway traffic past his bedroom door to the bathroom. He kept listening for a lull in the bathroom use so that he could get a turn. But people kept flowing in and out of that bathroom. Finally, just as he was getting desperate, there was a lull, so he dashed in. No sooner had he locked the door than one of the older children, who was late for work and thought it was a sibling inside, started pounding on the door, shouting, "Hey, you *know* no one is supposed to lock this door!" (The house rule regarding the bathroom door, made by the kids themselves, was that it shouldn't be locked. In order to get more use out of the bathroom at prime time, a room divider had been purchased.) Poor Uncle Marvin! He hasn't gotten over the shock of mornings at our house yet. He sighed, "No wonder the hallway carpet is wearing out. You've got more traffic here than they have at a Howard Johnson motel!"

Once we got over the embarrassment of having Uncle Marvin yelled at, we could laugh at ourselves. He's enjoyed telling the story more than once. Having guests and nesters around the house does add spice and humor—if only we remember to look for it.

In Conclusion

Nesting has been an unrecognized phenomenon in our day. Many people don't accept the idea because it can cause tension. However, there are many advantages to nesting and millions of families are keenly aware of this fact. These parents and grown children are sharing the same roof and reaping the benefits of a fuller life.

Notes

Chapter I

[1] As cited in Goodman, Ellen. "Together Again." *Boston Globe* Newspaper. Boston, MA. November 18, 1980. Editorial page.

[2] Cary, Lorene. "The Return of the Prodigals." *Time* Magazine. October 13, 1980, p. 118.

[3] Goleman, Daniel. "Leaving Home." *Psychology Today* Magazine. August, 1980. p. 53.

[4] Cary.

[5] Harris, Louis. "Good Family Life Tops American Priority List." *St. Paul Pioneer Press* Newspaper. St. Paul, MN. January 2, 1981, p. 1.

[6] Azzarone, Stephanie. "You Can Go Home Again." *San Francisco Chronicle* Newspaper. San Francisco, CA. December 17, 1980. p. EE-1.

[7] Lasch, Christopher. *Haven in a Heartless World, The Family Beseiged.* Basic Books, New York, NY. 1977. p. 5.

[8] Aries, Phillippe. *Centuries of Childhood.* Knopf. New York, NY. 1962. p. 411.

[9] Ibid.

[10] Ibid., p. 25.

[11] Goleman, p. 57.

[12] Goodman, Ellen.

[13] Weinstein, Grace. "Declaration of Independence." *Glamour* Magazine. August, 1980. p. 64.

[14] Goodman, Elaine and Walter. *The Family: Yesterday, Today, and Tomorrow.* Farrar, Straus and Giroux. New York, NY. 1975. p. 10.

[15] MacKenzie, Robert. "Review: 'I'm a Big Girl Now.' " *TV Guide.* February 21, 1981. p. 32.

[16] Ranieri, Ralph. "Getting Along with Adult Sons and Daughters." *Liguorian* Magazine. November, 1980. pp. 44-48.

[17] Wernick, Robert. *The Family.* Time-Life Books. New York, NY. 1974. p. 88.

[18] Goleman, p. 53.

[19] Wernick, p. 88.

[20] Cary.

[21] Phil Donahue Transcript #10280. Multimedia Program Productions. Cincinnati, OH. p. 33.

[22] Ibid.

[23] Ibid.

Chapter II

[1] As cited in Kett, Joseph. *Rites of Passage*. Basic Books. New York, NY. 1977. p. 127.

[2] Laslett, Peter, *The World We Have Lost*. Charles Scribner's Sons. New York, NY. 1965. p. 228.

[3] Victor, Joan Berg and Sander, Joelle. *The Family. The Evolution of Our Oldest Human Institution*. Bobbs-Merrill. Indianapolis/New York. 1978. p. 72.

[4] Ibid.

[5] Laslett, Peter and Wall, Richard. *Household and Family in Past Times*. Cambridge University Press. New York, NY. 1972. p. 306.

[6] Laslett, p. 92.

[7] Laslett and Wall, p. 370.

[8] Ibid., p. 369.

[9] Ibid., p. 408.

[10] Ibid., p. 372.

[11] Laslett, p. 83.

[12] Ibid., pp. 88-89.

[13] Russell, Josiah Cox. *Late Ancient and Medieval Population*. Transactions of the American Philosophical Society. Philadelphia, PA. 1958 v. 48, part 3, p. 31.

[14] Laslett, p. 90.

[15] Wernick, Robert. *The Family*. Time-Life Books. New York, NY. 1974. p. 43.

[16] As cited in Saveth, Edward N. "The Problem of American Family History." *American Quarterly* Periodical. 1969. p. 318.

[17] Ibid.

[18] Victor and Sander, p. 63.

[19] Goodman, Elaine and Walter. *The Family: Yesterday, Today, and Tomorrow*. Farrar, Straus, Giroux. New York, NY. 1975. p. 43.

[20] Wernick, p. 47.

[21] Victor and Sander, p. 48.

[22] Rhoads, Geraldine. "WD Doings." *Woman's Day* Magazine. November 25, 1980. p. 18.

[23] Victor and Sander, pp. 39-41.

[24] Goodman, p. 27.

[25] Wernick, p. 109.

[26] Phil Donahue Transcript #10280. Multimedia Program Productions. Cincinnati, OH. p. 17.

Chapter III

[1] Bombeck, Erma. "Grown Children Refuse to Leave Home Permanently." *Daily Camera* Newspaper, Boulder, CO. February 6, 1981. p. 13.

[2] Brooks, Andree. "When Married Children Come Home to Live." *New York Times* Newspaper, New York, NY. January 19, 1981. p. B10.

[3] Billings, Victoria. "Leaving Home vs. Living with Parents." *Glamour* Magazine. June, 1979. p. 102.

[4] Unidentified Phone-In Caller, *Twin City Today* Radio Show, Minneapolis, MN. December 10, 1980.

[5] Cary, Lorene. "The Return of the Prodigals." *Time* Magazine. October 13, 1980. p. 118.

[6] Phil Donahue Transcript #10280. Multimedia Program Productions. Cincinnati, OH. p. 36.

[7] *The U.S. Fact Book*. The Statistical Abstract of the United States. Bureau of Census, Department of Commerce, 98th Edition. New York, NY. Grossett & Dunlap. 1978.

[8] Cicero, Linda and Sonsky, Steve. "A Good Mate Is Hard to Find." *The Miami Herald* Newspaper. Miami, FL. February 8, 1981. Sec. G, p. 1.

[9] Ibid.

[10] *U.S. Fact Book*.

[11] Herskovits, Melville. *Cultural Anthropology*. Alfred A. Knopf. New York, NY. 1947. p. 170.

[12] Cicero and Sonsky.

[13] Ibid.

14 Ibid.

15 Wellemeyer, Marilyn. "Hubie Clark's Clan Kicks Up Their Heels." *Fortune* Magazine. August 11, 1980. pp. 80-94.

16 Ibid.

17 As cited in Baker, Ann. "The Family That Love Built." *St. Paul Sunday Pioneer Press* Newspaper. St. Paul, MN. December 14, 1980. Accent Section p. 1.

18 Bombeck.

19 Langway, Kirsch, and Hewitt. "Flying Back to the Nest." *Newsweek* Magazine. April 7, 1980. p. 86.

20 Ibid.

21 Laslett, Peter and Wall, Richard. *Household and Family in Past Times.* Cambridge University Press. New York, NY. 1972. p. 562.

Chapter IV

1 Harris, Sydney. "Parents Aren't Rational About Kids and Here's the Reason Why." *Chicago Sun Times* Newspaper. Chicago, IL. February 6, 1981. Editorial page.

2 As cited in Goleman, Daniel. "Leaving Home. Is There a Right Time to Go?" *Psychology Today* Magazine. August, 1980. p. 53.

3 Marcia, James. Simon Fraser University of British Columbia, Canada, as cited in "Leaving Home. Is There a Right Time to Go?"

4 Goleman, Daniel. "Leaving Home. Is There a Right Time to Go?" *Psychology Today* Magazine. August, 1980. p. 55.

5 As cited in White, Kate. "On Your Own." *Glamour* Magazine, October, 1979. p. 106.

6 As cited in Billings, Victoria. "Leaving Home vs. Living with Parents." *Glamour* Magazine. June, 1979. p. 102.

7 Weinstein, Grace. "Declaration of Independence." *Glamour* Magazine, August, 1980. p. 61.

8 Goleman, pp. 56 &57.

9 Ibid., p. 53.

10 Phil Donahue Transcript #10280. Multimedia Program Productions. Cincinnati, OH. pp. 40 &41.

11 Goleman, pp. 53 & 54.

12 Weinstein, p. 61.

[13] Comer, Nancy and Quinby, Brie. "Bringing Your Boyfriend Home." *Mademoiselle* Magazine. November, 1980. p. 200.

[14] Harris.

[15] Brooks, Andree. "When Married Children Come Home to Live." *New York Times* Newspaper. New York, NY. January 19, 1981. p. B10.

[16] Weinstein, p. 61.

[17] Ibid., p. 64.

[18] Koral, April and Glassman, Carl. "Are You Your Own Person or Your Parents'?" *Weight Watchers* Magazine. February, 1981. p. 7.

[19] Lambert, Shirley Taylor. *Farm Journal* Magazine.

[20] Rainieri, Ralph. "Getting Along with Adult Sons and Daughters." *Liguorian* Magazine. November, 1980. p. 47.

[21] Ibid., pp. 45 & 46.

[22] White, Kate. "On Your Own." *Glamour* Magazine. October, 1979. p. 106.

[23] Graham, Jory. "Friend's Death Means Beginning Anew." *St. Paul Dispatch* Newspaper. St. Paul, MN. April 4, 1981.

[24] As cited in Weinstein, Grace. "Declaration of Independence." *Glamour* Magazine. August, 1980. p. 64.

[25] Bombeck, Erma. "Kids Grow Up Only When Their Parents Permit It." *St. Paul Pioneer Press* Newspaper. St. Paul, MN. June 14, 1981.

[26] Donahue, p. 25.

[27] Goleman, p. 60.

[28] Cole, John N. "Leaving Home." Blair and Ketchum's *Country Journal* Magazine. February, 1979. pp. 77-81.

[29] Donahue, p. 19.

[30] Langway, Kirsch, & Hewitt. "Flying Back to the Nest." *Newsweek* Magazine. April 7, 1980. p. 86.

[31] Koral & Glassman. p. 7.

[32] Ibid.

[33] Ibid., p. 8.

[34] National Institute of Health study, as cited in "Leaving Home. Is There a Right Time to Go?" p. 59.

[35] Ibid.

Chapter V

[1] As cited in Baker, Ann. "The Family That Love Built." *St. Paul Sunday Pioneer Press.* St. Paul, MN. December 14, 1980. Accent Section. p. 1.

[2] Fast, Julius. *Body Language.* M. Evans & Co. New York, NY. 1970. p. 16.

[3] Ibid., p. 10.

[4] Ibid., p. 51.

[5] Ibid., p. 82.

[6] Vital Statistics of U. S. Government. Dept. of Health and Human Services. 1976 & 1977.

[7] *The U.S. Fact Book*, from the Statistical Abstract of the United States as prepared by the Bureau of Census, Department of Commerce. Table 272. New York, NY. Grossett & Dunlap. 1980.

[8] Dearman, Nancy and Plisko, Valena. *The Condition of Education.* 1980 edition. National Center for Education Statistics.

[9] *Students, Graduates, Dropouts in the Labor Market.* October, 1978. Bureau of Labor Statistics.

[10] Brothers, Joyce, M.D. "Dr. Joyce Brothers Answers Your Questions." *Good Housekeeping* Magazine. May, 1981. pp. 122 & 124.

[11] Baker.

[12] Ibid.

[13] Wernick, Robert. *The Family.* Time-Life Books. New York, NY. 1974. p. 113.

[14] Baker.

[15] Brooks, Andree. "When Married Children Come Home to Live." *New York Times* Newspaper. New York, NY. January 19, 1981. p. B10.

[16] Baker.

Chapter VI

[1] Wernick, Robert. *The Family.* Time-Life Books. New York, NY. 1974. p. 43.

[2] Phil Donahue Transcript #10280. Multimedia Program Productions. Cincinnati, OH. p. 17.

[3] Ibid. pp. 2 & 3.

4 Cary, Lorene. "The Return of the Prodigals." *Time* Magazine. October 13, 1980. p. 118.

5 Bombeck, Erma. "Youth World Runs on a $2 Check." *St. Paul Sunday Pioneer Press* Newspaper. St. Paul, MN. June 7, 1981. Accent Section. p. 9.

6 Cary.

Chapter VII

1 Phil Donahue Transcript #10280. Multimedia Program Productions. Cincinnati, OH. p. 34.

2 Goodman, Elaine & Walter. *The Family: Yesterday, Today, and Tomorrow.* Farrar, Straus and Giroux. New York, NY. 1975. p. 77.

3 Cary, Lorene. "The Return of the Prodigals." *Time* Magazine. October 13, 1980.

Chapter VIII

1 Phil Donahue Transcript #10280. Multimedia Program Productions. Cincinnati, OH. p. 31.

2 Wernick, Robert. *The Family.* Time-Life Books. New York, NY. 1974. p. 108.

3 Ibid., p. 116.

4 Comer, Nancy and Quinby, Brie. "Bringing Your Boyfriend Home." *Mademoiselle* Magazine. November, 1980. p. 266.

5 Donahue, p. 30.

6 Baker, Ann. "The Family That Love Built." *St. Paul Sunday Pioneer Press* Newspaper. St. Paul, MN. December 14, 1980. Accent Section. p. 1.

7 Ranieri, Ralph. "Getting Along with Adult Sons and Daughters." *Liguorian* Magazine. November, 1980. p. 45.

8 Halpern, Howard. *Cutting Loose.* Simon & Shuster. New York, NY. 1976. p. 105.

9 Ibid., p. 114.

10 Ibid.

11 Ibid.

12 Donahue, pp. 31 & 32.

[13] Ibid., p. 11.

[14] Winship, Beth. "Balancing the Voices Saying, 'Do it!' " *St. Paul Dispatch* Newspaper. St. Paul, MN. April 20, 1981. p. 11A.

Chapter IX

[1] Langway, Kirsch, & Hewitt. "Flying Back to the Nest." *Newsweek* Magazine. April 7, 1980. p. 86.

[2] Cary, Lorene. "The Return of the Prodigals." *Time* Magazine. October 13, 1980. p. 118.

[3] Phil Donahue Transcript #10280. Multimedia Program Productions. Cincinnati, OH. p. 18.

[4] Goleman, Daniel. "Leaving Home. Is There a Right Time to Go?" *Psychology Today* Magazine. August, 1980. p. 56.

[5] Langway, Kirsch, and Hewitt.

[6] As cited in Brooks, Andree. "When Married Children Come Home to Live." *New York Times* Newspaper. January 19, 1981. p. B10.

[7] Ibid.

[8] Weinstein, Grace. "Declaration of Independence." *Glamour* Magazine. August, 1980. p. 64.

[9] Ibid.

Permission Credits

Ann Baker. "The Family That Love Built." St. Paul Sunday Pioneer Press. St. Paul, MN. December 14, 1980. Accent Section. p. 1. Used with permission.

Victoria Billings. "Leaving Home vs. Living With Parents." *Glamour* Magazine. June, 1979. p. 100. Copyright © 1979 by the Conde Nast Publications Inc.

Andree Brooks. "When Married Children Come Home to Live." *New York Times* Newspaper. New York, NY. January 19, 1981. p. B10. Used with permission.

Lorene Cary. "The Return of the Prodigals." *Time* Magazine. October 13, 1980. p. 118. Copyright © 1980 Time, Inc. All rights reserved. Reprinted by permission of *Time*.

Linda Cicero and Steve Sonsky. "A Good Mate is Hard to Find." *The Miami Herald* Newspaper. Miami, FL. February 8, 1981. Sec. G, p. 1. Used with permission.

John Cole. "Leaving Home." Reprinted by permission of Blair and Ketchum's *Country Journal*. Copyright © February, 1979. Country Journal Publishing Co., Inc.

Nancy Comer and Brie Quinby. "Bringing Your Boyfriend Home." *Mademoiselle* Magazine. November, 1980. p. 200. Copyright © 1980 by the Conde Nast Publications Inc.

Phil Donahue Transcript #10280. Courtesy of Multimedia Program Productions, Inc.

Julius Fast. *Body Language*. Copyright © 1970 by Julius Fast. Reprinted by permission of the publisher, M. Evans and Company, Inc. New York, NY. 10017.

Daniel Goleman. "Leaving Home. Is There a Right Time to Go?" Reprinted from *Psychology Today*. Copyright © 1980 Ziff-Davis Publishing Company.

Ellen Goodman. "Together Again." *Boston Globe* Newspaper. Boston, MA. November 18, 1980. Editorial page. Used with permission.

Walter and Elaine Goodman. *The Family: Yesterday, Today, and Tomorrow*. Farrar, Straus and Giroux. New York, NY. Copyright © 1975. Used with permission.

Jory Graham. "Friend's Death Means Beginning Anew." *St. Paul Dispatch* Newspaper. St. Paul, MN. April 4, 1981. Copyright © 1981 Universal Press Syndicate. All rights reserved.

Sydney Harris. "Parents Aren't Rational about Kids and Here's the Reason Why." *Chicago Sun Times* Newspaper. Chicago, IL. February 6, 1981. Used with permission.

Shirley Taylor Lambert. *Farm Journal* Magazine. Used with permission.

Langway, Kirsch & Hewitt. "Flying Back to the Nest." *Newsweek* Magazine. February, 1980. Copyright © 1980 by Newsweek, Inc. All rights reserved. Reprinted by permission.

Peter Laslett. *The World We Have Lost.* Copyright © 1965. Reprinted with permission of Charles Scribner's Sons.

Joan Berg Victor and Joelle Sander. *The Family. The Evolution of Our Oldest Human Institution.* Copyright © 1978. Used with permission of the publisher, The Bobbs-Merrill Company, Inc.

Grace Weinstein. "Declaration of Independence." *Glamour* Magazine. August, 1980, p. 61. Copyright © 1980 by the Conde Nast Publications Inc.

Marilyn Wellemeyer. "Hubie Clark's Clan Kicks Up Their Heels." *Fortune* Magazine. August 11, 1980. pp. 80-94. Copyright © 1980 Time, Inc. All rights reserved.